HOW CAN I BE HAPPY?

HOW CAN I BE HAPPY?
(and other conundrums)

Paul Griffiths
and
Martin Robinson

MONARCH
BOOKS
Oxford, UK & Grand Rapids, Michigan, USA

First published in the UK in 2012 by Monarch Books
(a publishing imprint of Lion Hudson plc)
Wilkinson House, Jordan Hill Road, Oxford OX2 8DR, England
Tel: +44 (0)1865 302750 Fax: +44 (0)1865 302757
Email: monarch@lionhudson.com
www.lionhudson.com

ISBN 978 1 85424 932 6 (Print)
ISBN 978 0 85721 296 2 (Kindle)
ISBN 978 0 85721 297 9 (epub)
ISBN 978 0 85721 298 6 (PDF)

Distributed by:
UK: Marston Book Services, PO Box 269, Abingdon, Oxon, OX14 4YN
USA: Kregel Publications, PO Box 2607, Grand Rapids, Michigan 49501

The text paper used in this book has been made from wood independently certified as having come from sustainable forests.

British Library Cataloguing Data
A catalogue record for this book is available from the British Library.

Printed and bound in Great Britain by Clays Ltd, St Ives plc

This book is dedicated to:

the curious mind,

the questioning soul,

the enquiring spirit,

and the searching heart.

Contents

Acknowledgments

The ability to ask questions is one of the greatest gifts of life. To have the opportunity to get agitated about some issue, to think about it and then to compose a question that is often reworked as others bump against it is a real pleasure.

For that reason, we want to thank all those who have helped shape our questions and challenged us with enquiries as we have written this book.

We are enormously grateful to our good friend Tony Collins at Monarch Books for his encouragement and insight in bringing *How Can I Be Happy?* to print.

We also want to thank Marc Owen, Sharon Lanfear, Kent Anderson, Sue Philips, Steve Jones, Julie Kite, Paul Knight, David Moss, Ashley Lovett, and the many others involved for provoking us to pursue greater clarity and for refusing to let us get away with too much ambiguity.

For us, life is far more of an adventure and far more fun when you get to travel through it in the company of others. To all those who have shared our journey in the past or are doing so now, we want to say thank you.

Introduction

This book is about puzzling questions! But not the questions that you might find if you took a Mensa test, bought a puzzle book, or were part of a pub quiz team. It is doubtful that any of these questions have ever been asked on *Mastermind*.

This is a book about life's puzzling spiritual questions. Some research was recently conducted on the questions being asked by those who were interested in spirituality. The people conducting the survey identified a number of questions that were frequently asked by those who were open to spiritual matters. They were questions that have often teased or tormented humankind.

In reflecting on the conclusions that these researchers put forward, along with the observations of mystics of long ago, we have added our own anecdotal evidence drawn from talking with countless numbers of people, and have identified six questions that people are being drawn to explore today.

These days, our friends, neighbours and colleagues are interested in questions about identity (Who am I?), God (If there is a God, what is he or she like?), destiny

(What happens after I die?), happiness (How can I be happy?), suffering (Why is there suffering in the world?) and the spiritual world (What is the spiritual world and how does it impact my life?).

Social researcher David Hay has commented that there is enormous interest today in spiritual issues. He has also observed that many of us struggle to find a vocabulary to frame or express the questions that are often just below the surface of our lives but don't always find a natural outlet for conversation or discussion.

Therefore, rather than present a series of set answers, what we have attempted in the following pages is to navigate the various questions that people today would like to ask but don't always have the opportunity to ask. There is no set answer on offer, but rather an invitation to explore with us what these questions might look like. This book is more about enabling us to discover and express what the questions are than about being able to recite a formalized answer.

This book is part of a six-session course called Puzzling Questions, which aims to provide a safe place for people to consider, reflect on and talk about some of the questions they are carrying.

Over recent years there has been a subtle shift

in why some people go to see their doctor. Not only do people go and talk to their GP about physical issues that they are aware of, but now individuals go with pastoral and spiritual issues that they are struggling with – things that are actually affecting their health. What we aim to do through Puzzling Questions (the course) is provide a place where individuals can gather together and talk with friends about the things that deeply concern them.

The authors have been shaped in their own perspectives by the life and teaching of Jesus, and it is on these points of reference that they draw throughout this book. These points of reference are there to provoke further questions, not to offer specific answers.

Happy exploring!

Chapter 1

Who am I?

Introduction

The media love a mystery, and one of the stories to hit the national press a few years ago featured a drama surrounding a middle-aged man who had been found wandering around a provincial town. The man had completely lost his memory and had absolutely no awareness of who he was or where he was from. Further intrigue was added when it was discovered that the man in question was a classically trained pianist. Despite the attempts of the media and those who lived in the locality where he was found, no one was able to identify this gentle stranger for some considerable time.

As medical research pushes its boundaries ever further, finding more and more strategies and solutions for many chronic conditions and acute illnesses, people are living longer. Inevitably this pushes up the incidence of dementia, as it occurs predominantly in older people. Those who have travelled along with a loved one living with dementia often say, when death eventually comes, "Oh, I lost her ten years ago." When someone doesn't recognize us, can't remember a particular place or incident, gets angry because we never visit when we came only yesterday afternoon, sits placidly at the after-show party asking when the concert will be starting – we begin to feel they have been taken away from us; they are not the same any more. Our memory, our story, our relationships, and our sense of place all knit together to create what we think of as a person. So who am I really? If I lose my memory, will the people who love me feel that they have lost me?

Most of us will never have to face the problem of a total memory loss, but the question of our identity – who am I at a deeper level; who is the real me? – is something that we wrestle with throughout our lives.

Sometimes when people go through bitter trauma – injury, bereavement, betrayal, divorce, radical surgery, severe bullying – they can experience a conviction that they have lost themselves; they feel changed beyond recognition, damaged beyond repair. Rebuilding their lives involves a personal reinvention:

things will never be the same again. It's a question of recalibrating identity – who am I now, after such a profound experience?

From a strictly biological perspective, I am mostly water with a smattering of minerals and a bundle of DNA. The sociologist would go beyond that to factor in my education, employment, race, gender, and family background. The supermarket where I buy groceries online has an electronic profile of all my favourite food and what I use to wash my clothes and my crockery. The Criminal Records Bureau knows if I have a conviction or caution against my name. The cosmetic surgeon thinks I am a challenge, and wants to try to make me look less like I am and more like the fashionable ideal.

But do any of them really know who I am? More importantly, how do I identify who I am?

An ID card may give government officials a great deal of information – name, address, date of birth, and the tracking numbers that give access to the data our personal history has generated – but it still doesn't encapsulate the real me. We are more than a bundle of data. If you want to know the real me, you need to understand what I long for, what I am afraid of, what I believe, whom I love, what makes me laugh. You need to know about my dreams and my disappointments, my sense of inadequacy and the things I am really proud of. You need to know what I am secretly hoping for – and even what makes me bored.

I am more than a body. I am more than the clothes I wear and the products I buy and the job I do and the place where I live and where I went to school. I am more even than my past and the things that have happened to me and that I have done. I am as unique as my thumbprint. There is no one (not even if I have an identical twin) quite like me in the entire world.

Some recent research conducted by Coventry Cathedral, which investigated the spiritual questions that people are asking, suggests that identity is a huge issue for a good percentage of the population. Even a reflection on our life story fails to give immediate answers to the troubling question of who the real "us" actually is. Some would suggest that it is the failure to resolve this issue that leads to the proverbial mid-life crisis – the moment that comes when we have achieved the basics in life, a home, a family, a job, a circle of friendship, and yet still something eludes us.

At one level this is a profoundly spiritual question, and even if we do not see ourselves as "religious people" with particular religious commitments, many of us are asking profoundly important spiritual questions.

Inthis chapter we are beginning with the conviction that we are spiritual people living in a material world. We are also working with the idea that exploring spiritual questions can potentially help us to formulate answers to the question that begins this chapter: Who am I?

A spiritual identity

You don't have to be a "religious" person to believe that there is a spiritual dimension to life and to our personal identity. In the world of management it is now recognized that there are three components that determine a leader's skill level: their IQ, their EQ, and their SQ.

Whereas at one time it was believed that a manager's ability was determined by their IQ – their intelligence quotient – this is no longer the case. Following initial research into people in management, management theorists suggested that a person's EQ – their *emotional intelligence* quotient – was of equal significance to their IQ. As Daniel Goleman pointed out, their EQ gave them the capability of developing other leadership styles. Most managers have at best two management styles (out of six commonly accepted types). Someone who has developed his or her emotional intelligence can add to that. And this has major benefits.

Today, the notion of a person's IQ and EQ has been further extended to include their SQ: their *spiritual intelligence* quotient, which works with their EQ and IQ to make them the people they are and can become.[1] Spirituality has entered the workplace as more and more employers have recognized the need to develop their workforce from a more holistic perspective.

This discovery that we are as much spiritual people as we are physical people should not surprise us. Over 70 per cent of the UK population believe in God or at least in some kind of spiritual force. Roughly the same number of people pray either regularly or from time to time. The research project we mentioned earlier discovered that one of the questions people often ask is, "What is the spiritual world and how does it impact my life?" That question itself says something about who we sense we might be – beings with a strong spiritual dimension. (We will return to the question of the spiritual world and its impact in chapter 6.)

Researchers have charted a growing interest in all

---

1   If it is possible to develop a person's EQ and their IQ, then the debate about whether "great leaders" are born or made is reignited.

things spiritual, with a significant change in the belief structures that people use to make sense of their lives and to interpret the world around them. At one level we shouldn't really be surprised at such a shift in opinion. The majority of people in the world think about life in spiritual terms and those of us in the Western world who have previously rejected a spiritual view of life are to some extent returning to the kind of human norm that has prevailed throughout our existence.

It is not that we don't have an important physical dimension to our existence. Our bodies matter and we need to take care of the physical. But in addition to our bodily existence we also have soul and spirit capacities. These are not separate elements but in an ideal world operate and interact healthily with one another. It might help to think of our souls as the essential us – the part of our being that expresses who we are – our personality, the real, ongoing us. Clearly, unlike the physical body, the soul cannot be seen, but its impact on what makes us human is very important.

In a similar way, our spirit is that part of us that enables us to engage with the spiritual. Just like the soul, the spirit part of us cannot be seen, but it gives us the ability to communicate with other spiritual things.

In particular, our human spirit enables us to encounter and be encountered by God.

The French philosopher Pascal noted that there is within each one of us a God-shaped space. That void is the emptiness that the human spirit feels as it sails through life, directionless and yet yearning for a place it cannot find. We were created to know and experience God through the routine of our daily lives and it is our spirit that enables this to happen. The spirit part of us is equipped to pick up the transmissions that God is sending. Research suggests that most of us have, at one time or another, connected with that sense that there is more to life than the merely physical. We may choose to ignore such experiences, to downplay them and even to forget them, but many of us have had them.

Shaped by God

Unlike our physical self, which can easily be measured, described and recognized, it is much more difficult to speak clearly about the spiritual dimension of our lives. Where might we look for help? One potential resource is to be found in the pages of the Bible. For those who follow the example of Jesus, the Bible has a special weight of authority. The wisdom encountered in its pages can speak with such startling and transformative force into our lives that it can be experienced as "the word of God", and the Bible is sometimes called just that. So, when Christians sit down with the question "What matters about how I have been made?", they look to the Bible for some map bearings as they explore this idea.

Here are some of the thoughts the Bible offers in helping us to understand the particular spiritual shape that God gives to us all:

- "God created man in his own image" (Genesis 1:27). The Bible at this point is using the term "man" as meaning "humankind". The very next sentence in the Bible says: "in the image of God he created him; male and female he created them." So we can be sure that the Bible teaches that, though men and women are very different from each other in all kinds of ways, they are both made equally "in the image of God". He has poured himself into us in every sense. That raises some further questions. Clearly, although we might be created in the image of God, we are not the same as God, so in what ways does the image of God find expression in who we are?

- "We are God's work of art, created in Christ Jesus to live the good life as from the beginning he had meant us to live it" (Ephesians 2:10, JB). The Bible is suggesting that God made you to put goodness into the world and to experience life as good. Thinking about ourselves as carrying the potential for goodness within us as part of our identity is potentially very significant.

- "For you created my inmost being; you knit me together in my mother's womb" (Psalm 139:13). How intimate is that! The odd bundle of likes and dislikes that is you; the idea that God shaped us, knows us and approves of us as unique creations of his; that God had a hand in all this. That psalm goes on to say, "I am fearfully [i.e. mind-blowingly] and wonderfully made." This means that each one of us has at our core our own unique, amazing spark of mystery – the thumbprint, the signature, of God. Body and soul, God made us: even though it is also true that we all mess up sometimes, we don't have to apologize for being us. The Creator of the universe made the person that is you and knew what he was doing way back at the earliest moment of your conception.

- "Can a mother forget the baby at her breast and have no compassion on the child she has borne? Though she may forget, I will not forget you! See, I have engraved you on the palms of my hands..." (Isaiah 49:15–16). The Bible gives us a picture of a God who will never give up on us, because we are precious to him. This is more than the pride an artist feels in a masterpiece: this can be called nothing other than love. Even if we feel inadequate or unimportant, even if our self-esteem is at rock bottom, we are precious to God. He cares about us. He has not forgotten us. Sometimes people find this hard to accept, even if they believe in God. Especially if our parents or schoolmates or work colleagues have treated us badly or unjustly, it can be hard to imagine that God sees us as precious. Try saying to yourself, just quietly, "I am precious in God's sight" – not just once but every now and then through the day for the next week or so. Notice how it makes you feel.

To be loved and know we are loved; to have someone be proud of us; to be precious to someone – these are things that bring security and optimism and self-respect. They give us hope for our lives. They help us to realize that we are of value. We are worth something. We matter. We have infinite worth. It is for all these reasons that Christians sometimes speak about their faith using the phrase "good news". Not only has God made us and shaped us; his ongoing concern for us helps us to find our ultimate purpose and identity as human beings.

Life to the max

The healthy notion that we are of immense value can sometimes be strangely misdirected. Healthy people have a homing instinct for fun. In times of recession, chocolate sales buck the trend, as consumers search out a feel-good treat they can still afford. Having fun changes our body chemistry, our levels of dopamine and serotonin rising as we engage in some activity that we love to do. Exhilaration has been shown to be of immense benefit to the well-being of the immune system. Basically, we were born to savour life – a samba beat for life is wired into our DNA.

Like a plant that turns to grow towards the light, like insects that fly in from the night when the lamps are lit, so human beings are drawn towards happiness and well-being. As the human race goes on the quest for happiness, some people hit the jackpot while others end up in destructive blind alleys. Drugs, excessive drinking, and addictive shopping (and the debt that follows) are common ways to ruin a life in search of a good time. People addicted to sex, flitting from partner to partner and watching porn movies on the TV, experience the curious inverse ratio phenomenon – the more they grab, the less satisfied they end up. It seems we have to look for happiness in the right places.

What makes *you* happy? Looking back, can you identify moments when you have felt completely at peace, or completely content, or completely fulfilled? What gives you a real buzz – not a momentary high or thrill, but a real wow from head to toe?

Some people just wait to be happy: they believe happiness is not something you can command or control; you have to wait for it to alight like an elusive butterfly on your shoulder – maybe it will and maybe it won't. Others believe in working towards happiness: putting up with hardship and stringency now to attain a future goal. Some suggest that happiness is not a destination but the path you walk – that being happy is a choice and a decision you have to make every day.

For some at least, the life that they anticipate when they are young can go very wrong and prove to be full of major disappointments. How many people find the idea behind U2's song "I Still Haven't Found What I'm Looking For" a daily reality? The spiritual dimension to life tells us that we are made for more than disappointment – that we *can* find what we are truly looking for. Happiness and identity are in fact strongly connected. Knowing who we truly are is an important stepping stone towards the happiness that flows from deep contentment.

One of the most-watched programmes on UK television for many years was *One Foot in the Grave*. Its episodes followed the daily adventures of one of life's grumpiest characters. His approach to life ensured that he brought a rain cloud of depression wherever he went. With the catchphrase "I don't believe it!", Victor Meldrew was a very grumpy old man.

In the book of Ecclesiastes, King Solomon writes his musings on life, the universe and everything. "What's it all for?" he asks himself. Near the beginning of the book, in chapter 3 (verses 12 and 13), he says: "I know that there is nothing better for people than to be happy and to do good while they live. That each of them may eat and drink, and find satisfaction in all their toil – this is the gift of God" (TNIV).

Solomon is also credited with writing the book of Proverbs and a glorious, sensual celebration of love, the Song of Solomon. When we read the things he has written, we find ourselves getting to know a man who questions everything, who knows what it is to feel despair and disillusionment, even to be weary of life – but who also rejoices in beauty and love and the good things of this earth. He is not a shallow man; he is richly, intensely alive.

As St Irenaeus put it in the second century: "The glory of God is a human being fully alive." This is when we begin to see the connection between genuine happiness and the discovery of our true nature and purpose. We were made to be happy. Happiness is not about the quantity of life but the quality of life – a life well lived rather than a life satiated with desire. So what stops us from living such a life? Why should this not be straightforward?

Somehow we sense that things are not quite right

However you access the news, whether by television, radio, newspaper, or the internet, it can be a depressing experience. Granted, the news industry specializes in drama, crisis, and bad news. As one newspaper owner put it, "Good news doesn't sell newspapers." But even allowing for the bias of the media, it doesn't take much imagination to know that the world can be a pretty bleak place. The bad news that we see in real life is often mirrored in soap operas, films, and dramas of many kinds, even in novels.

The fact that there are many ugly situations in life and some very twisted individuals around could be written off as the exception. We are also aware that good people exist, that acts of kindness take place, that there is news to cheer the soul. And yet, it is hard to escape the feeling that there is a fatal flaw in life, that somehow a fault or fissure goes right to the heart of human nature. In fact, as we contemplate it further, we know that that same flaw is not far from the surface within our own being.

A spiritual perspective on life suggests to us that,

just as on a morning when you wake up with a stiff neck, so we all lead lives where things are "not quite right". There is an important sense in which we have all experienced some spiritual injury that has put us out of sorts with life. Because we are whole beings – body, soul and spirit – this injury to one part of us – our spirit – can have an impact on every part of who we are, in turn affecting each part of our daily life.

The debilitating results of our injury affect our relationship with God and our interactions with the world in which we live, with others, and even with ourselves. With regard to God, we sense that we have been unable to have an intimate relationship with him. We might know about him, and encounter him from a distance, but not know his nearness.

The impact of what we are describing as spiritual injury is far-reaching. Relationships can break down. There are families where people do not talk to each other, communities where you can't walk in certain places, and countries where particular people groups are harmed. If we weren't spiritually injured, Oprah's friend Dr. Phil would be out of work!

The high ideals we had for ourselves we do not always maintain, and the life we expected does not always come to fruition. We carry a sense that things are somehow just not quite right. It's hard to put our finger on what exactly is wrong, and yet we know intuitively that there is a problem. Even when we do have positive experiences, perhaps even achievements that we have dreamed of for years, when they actually come to us they don't always deliver exactly what we expected, and we can be left with a sense that we still haven't found the fulfilment we desired.

The sense of "gap" or "injury" that we have been describing can be addressed by restoring the spiritual part of our being. It takes courage, and possibly even strength, to grapple with the spiritual part of who we are, but realistically this is what is required to be in touch with who we really are – to be whole as people.

Made for eternity

The question of our identity, of who we are, inevitably raises some uncomfortable questions. Even our ability to think about our own existence allows us to ask about our *non*-existence. Where were we before we were born? Did we have any kind of existence, even as an idea in the mind of God, before we were born?

What happens to us when we die? Even if there is a life after death, a heaven of some kind, how is continuity with who we are now maintained? How do we remain recognizably the same person?

Another way of approaching that same question is to ask what the connection might be between life on this earth and life in eternity. The old Anglo-Saxon stories told of life on earth as being similar to a bird flying through a warm and well-lit feasting hall. The bird flies in from the darkness, briefly experiences warmth and human society, and then exits once more into the dark.

That's a rather bleak way of thinking about any continued existence. But supposing that our existence does continue and that beyond this life we find deep fulfilment? Might it be possible to draw some of that later life forward into this life? We reflected earlier that we were body, soul and spirit. Although our bodies are mortal, our soul and spirit are eternal. There will never be a day when we are not.

King Solomon, writing in the book of Ecclesiastes,[2] talks about the fact that God has set eternity within our hearts. In other words, there is within each one of us a

---

2   You can read more about what Solomon had to say on life in Ecclesiastes by reading Paul Griffith's book on it: *God on Life: An Ancient Guide to Living*, Carlisle: Authentic, 2003.

sense that our existence is far more than simply what we have here, our three score years and ten. There is a sense that we should live for ever. The poet Keats might have wanted to draw attention to the fleeting nature of life in his chosen epitaph, "Here lies one whose name was writ in water", but most of us realize that there is an impulse within us that wants to question that perspective.

Solomon says that although eternity is set in our hearts, we still can't fathom what God has done from beginning to end. It's as though we have a spark of mystery, but there is so much more to the Mystery than we can comprehend. It's as though we have what can only be called a soul, but our soul yearns for, reaches out for, looks up to Something or Someone beyond and above, which feels like home to us, which we recognize even though we don't have words to express it.

A sense of a connectedness to eternity can help us to figure out who we really are and what we were really made for. It might be possible to live now in the light of eternity.

Conclusion

We have looked in this chapter at who we are. As we have done so we have seen that we are individuals who are created by God, spiritual beings, made for eternity, built for enjoyment but also spiritually injured. We want to close this chapter by suggesting that we are also those who need to be rescued.

While filming a feature for the UK television car show *Top Gear* in 2006, presenter Richard Hammond was seriously injured as he attempted to record the maximum speed of a jet-powered car. In earlier times someone involved in such a horrendous accident would not have survived. It was a close call for Richard Hammond. He was badly hurt but, fortunately for him, as soon as the accident happened there were people present who could get him out of the car. After he had been cut from the car there was an air ambulance on hand to take him from the scene of the accident to hospital. When he arrived at the hospital there were people who could give him the physical care he needed. He continued on the road to recovery because he also received good quality aftercare. He was rescued and brought to a place of healing.

From the perspective of our spiritual selves we are immensely valuable and precious, but also injured or damaged. The point about exploring a relationship with God is to recognize our intrinsic worth and also to receive rescue and healing at the points in our life where injury has occurred.

The difficult part of such a message is that we need to accept our vulnerability and even helplessness in the face of spiritual damage. Richard Hammond, clever, able and healthy as he was, at the moment of the car crash was unable to help himself. Part of developing the spiritual life means being open to being helped, even to the point of looking to God to provide some rescue in our situation.

In this chapter, we've recognized that, though each of us has a value beyond price, we are also flawed – injured. We have gone through times when our lives have crashed; encountered situations we simply didn't know how to fix. Which of us hasn't, in some lonely moment, whispered: "Help me!"?

As we ask questions, as we explore the Mystery at the heart of life, as we probe to find the Something or Someone that lies beyond and behind the everyday, sometimes we get an odd sense of Something or

Someone looking right back at us – a hand grasps our hand as we reach out into the dark.

Chapter 2

What is God like?

Introduction

God is back.[3] The arresting title of a recent book draws attention to the fact that interest in God, faith, and religion in general is rising around our world. Contrary to the European view that religion and God would gradually fade from people's immediate horizon and even memory, the exact reverse has taken place.

In one way this is not too surprising. As we indicated in the previous chapter, people have always believed in God, and even in the UK belief in God has never fallen below 70 per cent of the population and arguably is closer to 90 per cent. However, when we get to the question, "What do people believe about God?", the answers become less clear. There seems to be a wide range of ideas about who God is and what he might be like.

Some see God in the traditional Christian

3   John Micklethwait and Adrian Wooldridge, *God is Back: How the Global Rise of Faith is Changing the World*, London: Allen Lane, 2009.

framework – God as a loving Father – but many have a much more tentative idea of what the term "God" means. God can mean a vague spirit, an invisible force, nature itself (Gaia), or simply an unknowable and distant deity impossible to describe.

For some people, the God who is not known is a God to be wary of. The idea that somehow God is out to get us is not uncommon. How do we avoid God's malevolent attention? We touch wood, we engage in a variety of other superstitious rituals, possibly without thinking too deeply about what we are doing, but somehow, in the background, there is a feeling that God is none too friendly.

What we believe about God matters. Just recently, there was a television debate on the BBC between an Anglican bishop and a range of adherents of some newer religious movements, which revealed a fascinating clash of views. There was huge disagreement whenever the discussion turned to aspects of personal behaviour. Eventually one panel member cried out in frustration: "Bishop, you keep talking about ethics. What has religion got to do with ethics?"

That was an interesting question, because historically there is an essential and necessary link between religion and ethics. It is precisely that link that is made in the pages of the Bible.

As people became more aware of who God was, so there was an expectation that there would be a change in the way that they lived – a change for the better. Encountering God was about discovering freedom, journeying on to become all that you were created to become. Among many other positive qualities, encountering God involved learning how to party and how to forgive others.

We can best arrive at an understanding of what God is like by focusing on some of the character attributes that are revealed through the encounters that people have had with God.

So what *is* God really like? What are his key character traits?

God is love

In some ways, this is the obvious character trait to begin with, and yet it is also a controversial place to start. It is not everyone's view of God. Those who have encountered huge tragedy in their lives sometimes blame God and tend to see him more as angry, vengeful, punishing, and even violent.

But Jesus, who had a lot to say about what God was like, is certain that God is love, so let's suspend judgment for a moment and explore what we mean by "love". In some ways "love" is a difficult word in English simply because we stretch it to cover a wide range of emotions and experiences. We use "love" to describe romantic love and even erotic love – those deep and passionate emotions that drive lovers to do foolish things and to make huge commitments to each other.

We also use "love" to describe the affection that we have for our immediate family members, or for our deepest friendships. There are people, especially those that we have known for a long time, of whom we can appropriately say that we love them. If they should become ill, we are deeply concerned for them. If they were to die, we might be devastated. These people who are close to us matter to us. That is obviously different from erotic love, but it's still love.

Then there is that other kind of love that we might even display towards those we don't really know well, but for whom we perform acts of kindness. We have no obligations towards these people, no family ties and no need to repay them for anything, and yet we are willing to be kind on occasion. That is also an important kind of love. It's the sort of love that, we might say, makes the world go round. We want to live in communities where people are kind to each other.

With all that in mind, what does it mean to say that God is love? The Bible paints a picture of a God who loves us in all these different ways. He wants to exercise kindness towards us; he desires to draw us into a deep relationship of a kind that we might describe as friendship. He wants an intimacy with us that some passages of Scripture suggest is the kind of passionate love that we might reserve for our spouse. We are his creation and, more than that, his children, for whom he cares deeply.

The love that is part of the character of God is something that is never switched off. It is offered whether it is deserved or not. It is gracious or undeserved love, freely offered whatever our actions might be.

Those who claim to have experienced the loving character of God often demonstrate that such an experience is transformative. It has an impact on their future lives. Having been loved, somehow they can't help loving others.

Perhaps one of the most famous examples of the love of God producing love for others is to be found in the life of Mother Teresa, the founder of the Missionaries of Charity. She deliberately chose to orientate her work towards, in her own words, "the hungry, the naked, the homeless, the crippled, the blind, the lepers, all those people who feel unwanted, unloved, uncared for throughout society, people that have become a burden to the society and are shunned by everyone".

These were precisely the people who could give nothing back to her. She became most famous for giving dignity to those whom nobody else cared about – the dying poor. It seemed almost a senseless act to take in those who were at death's door, whose lives could not be saved, and simply to give them some dignity in the last few days or hours of life. If those whom her sisters took in were Muslims, then they were read the Koran in their last days of life. Those who were Hindus were given water from the Hindu sacred river, the Ganges, while those who shared her own faith were given the last rites. In every case they were given a taste of the love of God, we might even say a practical experience of the character of God.

Malcolm Muggeridge made a famous BBC

documentary on the remarkable story of Mother Teresa with the title *Something Beautiful for God*. Muggeridge was even then on his own journey from a well-known and radical atheism towards becoming a Christian. His encounter with Mother Teresa formed a significant part of that journey. In the book that flowed from the documentary he commented that what had made the biggest impression on him was the sight of young nuns, previously from high-caste Hindu backgrounds, now converted to Christianity, working with the poorest of the poor. They were touching, washing and caring for those whom in the past they would have been required to shun. This spoke loudly to Muggeridge of the astonishing power of the love of God.

From the earliest days of Christianity, the desire to offer practical care to others has been inextricably linked to the spread of the faith. Wherever Christians go, they establish charities that offer practical care. It's not an instruction but an intuitive response to the love of God. It's not that you have to be a Christian to love others, but rather that it's hard to be a Christian and *not* express love. It comes with the territory, and if it doesn't you can be sure that something is wrong that needs to be put right.

God loves justice

It has sometimes been suggested that the image of God portrayed in the first half of the Bible (the Old Testament) is different from the description of God presented in the second half (the New Testament).

It's easy to have the impression that the God of the Old Testament is an angry and vengeful God and the God of the New Testament is a God of love. There certainly are references to the anger of God, particularly in the Old Testament. What is it that makes God angry? Essentially, God gets angry about injustice and particularly when the poor, the defenceless, the weak and the marginalized are mistreated.

God seems to have a special regard for those who are often in these categories: widows, children, orphans, the elderly, and foreigners – all the people who are easily overlooked and essentially without power and influence. God becomes angry when injustice is meted out to these kinds of people.

When we see the people and issues towards which God's anger is directed, we can see the connection between his anger and his love. If you love people, you naturally become angry when they are mistreated. Love and indignation about injustice are not opposite sides of a schizophrenic God; they are naturally and essentially connected dimensions of his character.

The story of the Bible contains many accounts of the indignation of God over issues such as the bribing of judges so that the poor cannot obtain justice, the fiddling of weights and measures so that people don't receive a fair deal, the piling-up of debts such that the debt becomes crippling and can't be repaid and – possibly more than any other single thing – God cares about the mistreatment of children.

When God spoke through one of his designated spokespeople he usually focused on issues of justice, and passages like this are commonplace:

> *Woe to those who make unjust laws, to those who issue oppressive decrees, to deprive the poor of their rights and withhold justice from the oppressed of my people, making widows their prey and robbing the fatherless.*
>
> *Isaiah 10:1–2*

This is when we begin to see that the connection between ethics and religion matters a great deal, and that the character of God is what secures that essential connectivity. Again, it seems to be the case that when men and women experience the God of justice they too want to work for justice.

John Newton, the author of the famous hymn "Amazing Grace", was once a notorious slave trader. After he became a Christian, he left that business and became a well-known preacher and vicar in London. It took some time, but eventually he began to think about how slavery might be abolished. One of those he influenced was a new and young member of parliament, who had himself recently become a Christian. His name was William Wilberforce. It became Wilberforce's life's work to end the practice of slavery, not just in the United Kingdom but throughout all the lands and territories where Britain had either rule or influence. Eventually the Royal Navy became an important enforcer of justice, acting against the slave trade internationally.

In a later generation, Martin Luther King Junior took up the cause of civil rights on behalf of the descendants of slaves. He had been influenced by the faith of his father, like him also a Christian minister. Luther King Junior drew heavily upon his Christian faith and the images of justice that he found in the Old Testament. The exodus of the people of Israel from slavery in Egypt and their journey to a promised land became a powerful theme in his imagination and in his preaching. In one of his final speeches, he alluded to the Promised Land and said, "I have seen the Promised Land. I may not get there with you. But I want you to know tonight, that we, as a people, will get to the Promised Land."

For Luther King Junior, the connection between justice and civil rights was obvious, and the connection between working for justice and the active service of others was just as clear. These are some of his words spoken on another occasion:

Everybody can be great. Because anybody can serve.

You don't have to have a college degree to serve.

You don't have to make your subject and your verb agree to serve.

You don't have to know about Plato and Aristotle to serve.

You don't have to know Einstein's theory of relativity to serve.

You don't have to know the second theory of

thermodynamics in physics to serve.

You only need a heart full of grace. A soul generated by love.

A God who is trustworthy

Recently some friends of ours celebrated their twenty-fifth wedding anniversary. There have been moments when life has not been easy for this couple, and yet despite the challenges they have decided not to give up on each other but rather to work through their very painful problems. When we caught a few minutes with them during their special day they expressed one of the reasons why after twenty-five years of marriage they were still together: they had made a promise to each other on their wedding day and they were determined to honour that promise for the rest of their lives.

In reading through the Bible, what you discover is that God is presented as someone who keeps his promises. Scripture describes God as faithful, and as such he is never going to give up on us and never stop trying to do the best he can for us. He can be trusted.

Trust is the basis of all good relationships, relationships that last. It is the basis of true love and beyond that it is the basis for that complexity of relationships that we might think of as community and, by extension, society itself. Some would argue that for a society and an economy to flourish there has to be a widespread sense that we can trust our neighbours, our colleagues and those with whom we do business. Commerce would in fact cease without a significant basis of trust in many of our core dealings and transactions.

That might sound a little far-fetched, but stop to think of the number of things that you take on trust, or take for granted, as you get up each day. We trust that the lights will come on when we flick a switch, that the news we hear on the television has some basis of truth, that the bus or train will be running more or less on time, that when we pay our fare our money will be accepted as legal tender. We can go on through our whole day describing a multitude of hidden trusts so familiar to us that we notice how basic they are only when they are withdrawn or betrayed.

It is for these reasons that the breaking of trust is so serious. To have your house burgled can be deeply disturbing. To feel that you can't walk the streets in safety is fundamentally corrosive. To be defrauded, to be lied to, to have people insist that nothing will happen unless we pay a bribe, to know that we stand no chance of winning a contract without a significant "donation" – all these contribute to the erosion of trust to the extent that society loses its glue, its health and its viability.

Recent studies have suggested that the single biggest factor in the ending of poverty in many countries is not simply to increase overseas aid so much as to encourage good governance. The ending of corruption and the building of trust is the key to a healthy society and a vibrant economy.

It becomes clear that being trustworthy is in fact another dimension of both love and justice. It helps to bind these elements together, to give them practical impact. For societies to be corruption-free there have to be trustworthy individuals in key posts.

The early part of the eighteenth century in England was noted as one that was deeply corrupt. The corruption began at the top and flowed down. Government posts were bought and sold, positions of many kinds were given to favourites, market forces were given free rein, the judiciary was capable of being bribed, and even the livings in Church of England parishes were up for sale.

In the middle of the eighteenth century England began a gradual change as the growth of the Methodist revival started to bring people whose lives reflected the trustworthiness of God into public life and especially into commerce. The notions that an Englishman's word is his bond and that high officials can be trusted, and the idea of honest public service as an expression of virtue, all stem from this time. That development was hugely beneficial to society as a whole. When honesty becomes the norm, then the rights of the poor, the weak and the disadvantaged begin to be guaranteed. That kind of outcome pleases God, because he is himself trustworthy.

God is a jealous God

In the midst of all this talk about love, justice, and trustworthiness comes an attribute of God that just doesn't seem to fit. Why should God, the all-loving, all-forgiving Father who goes on trying all the time for reconciliation, ever allow himself to be *jealous*?

Where do we get the idea that God is jealous in any case? If we turn to the Ten Commandments,[4] we find that the first few commandments are a bit surprising:

4   The Ten Commandments are a set of guidelines that God gave to help people live the best type of life possible; see Exodus 20.

I am the Lord your God, who brought you out of Egypt, out of the land of slavery. You shall have no other gods before me. You shall not make for yourself an idol in the form of anything in heaven above or on the earth beneath or in the waters below. You shall not bow down to them or worship them; for I, the Lord your God, am a jealous God, punishing the children for the sin of the fathers to the third and fourth generation of those who hate me, but showing love to a thousand generations of those who love me and keep my commandments. You shall not misuse the name of the Lord your God, for the Lord will not hold anyone guiltless who misuses his name.

The next commandment deals with the keeping of the Jewish Sabbath,[5] which could be construed as another commandment in which God is concerned with himself. The remaining six deal with everything else that we are to do with regard to our relationships with one another.

As one good friend put it to Martin, "Does God have an inferiority complex? Why is he so obsessed

---

5   The Jewish Sabbath was more than a day of rest (an old-fashioned Sunday). It was also about focusing on their relationships – with their immediate family, with the story of their ancestors, with the wider faith community and with the God whom they worshipped.

with the idea that everyone should worship him?"

These are good questions, and at first sight it does seem as though God has temporarily lost touch with all those other fine attributes that we have explored so far. However, on closer examination we discover that there is indeed a deep connection between God's love for us and his apparent desire to be worshipped. It is simply this: only God can be trusted with being worshipped. All other objects of worship will in the end deceive, damage or even destroy us.

It seems as though we are created to worship something or someone. As Bob Dylan's song title goes, we've all "Gotta Serve Somebody".

We might think we are independent, that we stand alone, but in reality there is always someone demanding something of us. We see it most clearly in what is called the "work–life balance". It's hard to escape the fact that our employers too often want more from us than they really deserve. Jesus puts it this way: "Give to Caesar what belongs to Caesar, and give to God what belongs to God" (Mark 12:17, NLT). The reality is that the Caesars in our lives always desire to take more than they deserve. God, however, treats us with respect and never demands more than he is entitled to.

Once we have accepted that we are all going to serve or worship someone or something, then the all-important question becomes, "Who or what is worthy of our service or worship?"

The recent collapse of some banking institutions in the UK, with the financial hardship that this has brought into people's lives, has resulted in an appropriate caution about where people put their money. In such difficult times the last thing that anyone wants is to be banking his or her hard-earned money recklessly.

This same sense of caution is encouraged in the pages of the Bible. But the sense of cautiousness is not so much to do with where we deposit our money as with where we invest our service and our worship. Not everything that sets itself up to be served or worshipped is good for us. The pages of the Old Testament are littered with the tragic events that follow for those who commit idolatry – who prioritize anything as more important in their life than God. In reality, anything that we worship other than the God who has made us has the potential to harm us.

What many have discovered is that false gods exact heavy penalties. However, those who seek to worship God discover that the God who loves us knows that we are made in such a way that we are complete only when worship of him is part of our lives. He knows too that only when we worship him will we come to no harm through the act of worship. In fact, quite the reverse: the worship of God is what brings us fulfilment, completion, true satisfaction, and contentment – what the Bible calls "blessing".

In the New Testament Jesus suggests that it is the poor in spirit who are most likely to inherit the kingdom of God;[6] it is those who are innocent (like children) who are most likely to see (perceive) God. Jesus calls them "blessed", which really means a curious mix between happy and fulfilled. The faithfulness and love of God draw us towards such a state of being blessed. Justice for the poor and the pure becomes a reality through such blessedness.

The creative God

The opening words of the Bible ("In the beginning God created...") make it clear that God is truly and

---

6   "The kingdom of God" was a phrase coined by Jesus to refer to a movement that he was leading and inviting people to belong to. It was often a "catch-all" phrase that described a different way of living and had something to do with the breaking through of the influence of God. It was a place where God reigned.

fundamentally creative. It is not just that he has learned some creative skills; his actual nature or character is to be creative. That single reality carries with it many implications. It doesn't take long for us to realize that God's creative nature contains a love for beauty. In fact, creative energies tend towards the production of beauty. Think for a moment about our beautiful planet – the unique blue-and-green planet, hanging in space, bathed in the light of the sun, unlike any other planet that we know about. As many space travellers report, it is an inspiring, possibly even awe-inspiring, sight viewed from a vantage point away from the earth itself.

The beauty of the planet viewed from space is echoed in every aspect of the natural world, on the earth, in the air and under the sea. Everything that the creator God has touched reflects beauty back to us. It's not difficult to think spiritual thoughts and to worship God silently when one is walking through the countryside in a whole variety of weather conditions. Even the rain and the fog have their own strange beauty.

When we witness all this natural beauty it's not difficult to see why the worship of God is associated with beauty in so many ways. When we build churches and cathedrals it is always an attempt to build something beautiful. Even apart from the actual design of the building, we like to fill worship space with beautiful artefacts. Whether it be stained-glass windows, paintings, gorgeous wall hangings, altar cloths, chalices or even the furniture we sit on, beauty and worship are naturally connected.

It is no coincidence that through the years the church has been a major patron of the arts: whether that art has been used to decorate churches, such as the roof of the Sistine Chapel, or to form sculptures outside churches, beautiful things speak to us of God. It's the same when we turn to music or speech: whatever form of art we might use, we associate creativity with the character of God.

The association with beauty also reflects God's interest in pleasure and playfulness. Jesus began his ministry on earth at a joyful wedding and many of his most important encounters occurred at feasts and festivals. Celebration seems to be written into the DNA of creation, and celebration draws us straight back into love, faithfulness, rejoicing in the good, worshipping the one who is true; into that which we have already mentioned – a sense of wonder and awe.

This is what God is like.

It is important to note here that many who met and knew Jesus of Nazareth came to believe that their encounter with him gave them an insight into what it would be like to know and meet God.

Chapter 3

What happens after I die?

Introduction

Martin's philosophy teacher was always fond of saying, "The rate of human mortality has remained remarkably constant throughout human history at 100 per cent." In short, we are all going to die, and along the way, whenever someone we know dies, we get a reminder of our own mortality. There is always a stark finality about a funeral service. Questions that we normally do not face can hardly be avoided.

If you have been present during someone's final moments, you will know that there is a very obvious sense that the person you knew is no longer there. All that is left is the body – a mere shell. The real person that you knew has truly departed. There comes a moment, when somebody dies in a hospital or hospice, after the long hours of rasping breath, when someone says "She's gone", and it is time to close her eyes, to wash her, to make the arrangements, and to commend her body to the elements or to the quiet keeping of the earth.

He or she has gone. So that raises the question: Where might they have gone to?

There is no getting round it: death is in a sense very final. Whatever we may believe, this chapter on earth, at least, has come to an end. The finality of death is the part that is obvious. What has come to an end is physical and visible, and it is the material aspects that must be wrapped up. The body must be disposed of, the bank accounts closed, the will read, and maybe a house sold or passed on. None of these are needed any more. But were any of those ever the real person?

What continues? Where and in what sense does any part of who we are continue? What kind of being shall we be? Will we still be individuals? Will our friends be able to recognize us again one day? How might we live on? These questions, at a time of bereavement, are not idle wondering: they burn; they acquire the sharpest urgency; if we never cared before, suddenly now we need to know. And, in bereavement, we often change our minds. Odd, inexplicable occurrences, flashes of insight and prescience – these set us wondering.

Dead end!

So what are the options? The obvious and somewhat bleak answer is that *nothing* happens. Death is simply the end. When the brain stops, we cease to exist. If we take that view, the priority for the living is to focus on the here and now, because "when you're dead you're dead". In other words, there is nothing else, no hope, no continuance; just nothing.

But many people do believe in some form of afterlife, so how might life continue after the body dies?

Though the body dies, and we can all see that it does, there are several senses in which our life may continue after death.

We live on in our families and those we have influenced

The scholar, teacher, and scout leader Forest E. Witcraft said: "A hundred years from now it will not matter what my bank account was, the sort of house I lived in, or the kind of car I drove... but the world may be different because I was important in the life of a child."

Even those who believe that there is no life after death, in any personal and individual sense, can easily see that each of us lives on in the body of work we have left, or the children born to us, or the way we have influenced others.

Some believe we return to the ocean of life

For those who do not believe in a personal deity, there is often a belief in what we might call "the ocean of life". This gives us the concept that our lives are each like a small wave on the surface of the ocean. The waves come and they go, are born and then die, each with their own individual, distinct, separate form: each one an expression of the great ocean, made entirely of that ocean. Each one is just a ripple on the top of something huge, going down to depths unimaginable. Each one has the resources of that great ocean of life; the same resources that inform and support all the others. And when each one dies, it is no more than a returning to that greater body of life, their source and their home, where they are at one with every other form of life.

Some believe we go to a world of light, our home

William Wordsworth's famous poem "Intimations of Immortality" says:

Our birth is but a sleep and a forgetting:
The Soul that rises with us, our life's Star,
Hath had elsewhere its setting,
And cometh from afar:
Not in entire forgetfulness,
And not in utter nakedness,
But trailing clouds of glory do we come
From God, who is our home.

There are many people who have been resuscitated, brought back after having technically died, who speak of an experience of travelling down a tunnel to a world of light. This experience of seeing light is often explained as being a physical effect created by nerves dying, but those who have come back from the threshold of death are often profoundly changed in outlook. Some who have undergone such an experience have nothing to report; others return transformed, with a more generous, appreciative, and relaxed outlook, feeling certain they have known a touch of the divine.

Some believe we return to a new life on earth

Julius Caesar described the Celts as fearless warriors, saying that the reason for this was that they wished to inculcate this as one of their leading tenets, that souls do not become extinct, but pass after death from one body to another.

Certainly the belief that when we die we go on to a life beyond this one, or will be born as a new body in this life, sometimes allows people to face death with greater tranquillity and acceptance.

This type of belief in reincarnation can be particularly comforting to those who have lost a child – whether an infant or a child not yet born. This belief system would identify such a situation as indicating that the child was a soul of such purity that he or she did not need to stay here very long; this brings a sense of privilege at having been chosen to share in that brief journey, and can be comforting in the grief of loss.

Some believe we go to a place of purification

In the Christian religion, one of the distinctions between the groups that can broadly be called "Catholic" and "Protestant" is the Catholic belief in the state known as "purgatory" – a time for the soul to be cleansed from sin[7] after death before entering heaven.

Purgatory is often spoken of as if it were a place – a bit like animals in quarantine between one country and another – but in reality it is understood to be a state of the soul, for "place" would imply time and space, neither of which applies to the world of spirit.

The tradition of purgatory suggests a period of cleansing – a transformation like a piece of metal being hammered out on the blacksmith's anvil – but it is the anteroom of heaven, and so overall is seen as a welcome step forward towards the home of God.

Some believe we go to heaven or hell

There is much diversity of belief in the Christian faith

7   Sin is defined as any attitude or act that is not an expression of all that we were created to be. God's dislike of it has more to do with the damage it causes us than with anything else.

community, but the Bible is always seen as a serious authority, most particularly the Gospels, which contain the teaching of Jesus. Therefore in the Christian faith tradition there has always been a strong consensus of belief in the reality of heaven and hell, because Jesus clearly believed in both.

Jesus also speaks vividly and graphically about hell, both in his parables and in his direct teaching. But the passages where he talks about hell are minor in comparison to his concern about how we live in this life. His teaching about this life is often described as the breaking through of the influence of God, or the reign of God. Jesus talks about the influence of God as the kingdom of God.

In the first four books of the New Testament we have a significant body of Jesus' teaching about the kingdom of God; some of it clearly relates to life here on earth, but some seems to look forward to a time to come, when the people of earth will be summoned into the presence of the God of heaven. The vocabulary used of that gathering is that of a party – a feast, a wedding banquet, a time of consummation and rejoicing.

According to Jesus, one of the determining factors in our being included in that heavenly banquet is whether we have treated others with humility, mercy, and compassion in this life – see his parable of the sheep and the goats in Matthew 25:31–46; also this passage in Matthew 7:21–23:

> *Not everyone who says to me, "Lord, Lord," will enter the kingdom of heaven, but only he who does the will of my Father who is in heaven. Many will say to me on that day, "Lord, Lord, did we not prophesy in your name, and in your name drive out demons and perform many miracles?" Then I will tell them plainly, "I never knew you. Away from me, you evildoers!"*

What might such an afterlife look like, and how do we make sense of concepts such as heaven and hell? Should we take the idea of hell seriously, or is it just an outmoded idea that our forebears used to frighten the wicked? One option is to believe that hell does not exist and that heaven is open for everyone. The argument runs that God loves us all and doesn't want anyone to suffer, and so no one is excluded from the all-embracing love of God – the door is thrown open to anyone who might want to walk through it.

It doesn't take much imagination to see that

there could be some problems with the idea that we all simply move from this life to another world. What about those who don't *want* to spend eternity in heaven? What flows from love soon becomes coercion. Is it then possible that heaven is only for some and not for all? Could it be the case that God is both loving and just, and has provided help for people to be rescued from their situation?

Because this can all sound complex and uncertain, it's tempting to live our lives in hopeful ignorance. We really don't know what is going to happen next, but we hope it will be OK.

Given that there are so many views about life beyond death, what would most Christians want to offer as hope for humanity?

Death is not the end, only a doorway

As the epic final part of Tolkien's Lord of the Rings trilogy, *The Return of the King*, draws to a close, we find its leading characters all gathering at the quayside. They are there to say goodbye to those who are about to catch the last ship to leave Middle-earth. It is a scene full of emotion and fond farewells, as those leaving on the ship know they can never return to those they are leaving behind. There is, however, a sense of peace and purpose in their final voyage.

This ship could be seen to represent our last journey here on earth – the idea is that death is our last great adventure as we sail to the world beyond. Death is not seen as the end, but purely as a voyage we must all travel as we head for that new life which is beyond the grave.

As we suggested in the first chapter, it's possible that we were all made for eternity. Therefore, death can be seen as nothing more than our wardrobe, through which we travel into C. S. Lewis's Narnia. Jesus is remarkably unforthcoming in descriptive detail when he speaks about eternity or heaven. But he is very clear that heaven is our destination should we desire it.

Apart from that penultimate scene from *The Return of the King*, the idea of death not being the end is expressed no better than in Gandalf's conversation with Pippin at Minas Tirith. On the eve of battle, Gandalf and the hobbit Pippin explore their thoughts about tomorrow. For Pippin there is only despair, as he sees death as the end. Yet Gandalf assures him that he should not be afraid of the outcome of the battle, for death is not the end of the journey: "It is but another path that we must all take. It is when the grey rain curtain of this world rolls back and all turns to silver glass and then... you see it – white shores and beyond that a far green country under a swift sunrise." It is a place of inconceivable beauty.

To reiterate what we expressed earlier, the key to perceiving that death is not the end is appreciating that we are eternal beings – built to live for ever. The reason that we experience physical death is our failure to fulfil the conditions of that eternal promise that God made to our ancestors. We will look a little more at what those conditions were and their impact on us in chapter 5.

One of the reasons people sometimes find funerals heartbreaking is the thought that they are saying goodbye for ever to the person who has died. The heartbreak of the immediate loss and loneliness is compounded by the realization that they will never be with that person again. According to St Paul and the other writers of the New Testament, however, death is not the end. At someone's funeral we are but uttering a fond adieu... until we meet again. That does not mean that grief should not be part of the funeral experience. Even if we expect to see our loved ones again, there still remains a legitimate sense of loss and loneliness as we continue to live this life without them.

Someone will meet you after death

Andrew's father-in-law recently retired. During his working life he was a very busy man, so in retirement he and his wife are making the most of their free time. Taking holidays is one of their primary pleasures. Over the last twelve months it seems to Andrew and his wife that his in-laws have spent nearly half the inheritance as they have travelled to Switzerland, Iceland, Madeira, Cornwall, and various other places!

All these trips have been with the same organization. When asked why they were always going with the same people – especially as you can get better deals with other companies – his in-laws said that their choice of travel company all boiled down to one factor: that the organization that they go with offers a tour guide. They like to have a designated person to look after them throughout their various trips.

As soon as they arrive at their destination there is someone there to meet them. It doesn't matter whether they arrive at the station, the airport or the dock; the company has representatives there to meet them. Having greeted them, the rep then shows them to their accommodation and for the length of their holiday will make sure that everything is just right for their enjoyment.

The teaching of Jesus suggests that, from the moment of death, there will be someone who meets you on the other side of death and takes responsibility for looking after you. That person will welcome you, that person will care for you, that person will guarantee your well-being. The New Testament suggests that we have the possibility of meeting Jesus on the other side of death.

If you know anything about tour guides you will know that there are certain qualities that you look for in a good one. They should be from the area that you are visiting, be of reliable character, and if at all possible be related to those who own the travel company. Family connections are best because this provides an extra motivation for your guide to care for you and the reputation of the company. This is pretty much how it is with Jesus being our guide.

Many years ago Paul was invited to head off to South Korea and speak at various churches. The people who organized the trip told him that they would be at the airport waiting for him when he arrived. When he landed, after what seemed a very long journey to a country that he had never been to before, where a language was spoken that he did not speak, he discovered that his hosts were not there. This was disappointing to say the least. How much better to have certainty about what might happen at the end of life's journey.

In the Hollywood epic *Braveheart*, the final scene sees William Wallace being hanged, drawn, and quartered outside the gates of the Tower of London. As he is experiencing indescribable pain he cries out with all the strength he can muster, "Freedom!" Unbeknown to those there watching, but real to Wallace, this strength is found because in his mind's eye he can see dancing in and out of the crowd the spirit of his sweetheart. His wife had been butchered at the hands of the English, but Wallace sees her coming to journey home with him. His body is being ripped apart, his life is coming to an end, and yet there she is coming to take his hand and bring him home.

The hope of those who follow the teachings of Jesus is that, as they travel through life and then ultimately through death, they do so in the company of Jesus.

A new body awaits us

About twelve months ago Elizabeth's husband died. He had been in the process of dying for the last five years or so. Near the end of his life, after having fought such a long and brave battle against his various ailments, the cost of his long illness had weighed heavily on his body. The year before he died he lost one of his legs, and by the time of death his body had withered terribly.

Jesus teaches that when we die we will receive a new body. Just what kind of body is not so clear, but certainly a body that is recognizably us. For Elizabeth's partner, what that means more than anything else is a new body free from disease, and the ability to walk and run and never be tired.

A little while ago a friend sent us a link to a website that does face recognition. The idea is that you upload a picture of your face to this website and it tells you which famous person you look like. When Paul did it, it told him that he looked like Ariel Sharon and a particular female tennis star! It offers you several options, all based on a percentage of how much you look like them.

Obviously, we can't know exactly what we will look like in heaven, but there is an indication in the Christian tradition that we will be recognizable and in some important ways reflect the image and character of the God who made us.

A popular TV programme in recent years has been *The Biggest Loser*. The idea of the series is to track the weight loss of several people who have been encouraged to lose as much weight as possible by diet and exercise. The person who loses the most weight is the biggest loser, and hence the winner.

A recent final included the three people who had lasted longest at the academy. In introducing each of these remaining contestants, the presenter reminded the audience what the competitors had looked like before they entered the programme. It would be fair to say that the audience was astonished by the transformation; they had, it seemed, been given a brand new body and yet it was also clear that they really were the same people. Continuity but improvement! That is the picture that the teaching of Jesus leaves us with. Our bodies will be the same but different!

A time of appraisal

The story is told of a businessman who had developed his business over many years. He had become a very successful man as he modelled a textbook example of how to grow your own little empire. He had invested slowly and wisely, and when the moment came that he was offered a great amount of money for his company he grabbed it with both hands – it was such a good deal that he just had to take it.

Rather than start another business or look for another job, this man decided finally to take the retirement that he had been talking about with his wife. After all those years of constant hard work, now was the time to sit back and enjoy life. Having got to know lots of people over the course of his working life, this man decided to throw a big retirement party at which he could mark the end of his working life and thank everyone he had known. Tragically, on the night of his big do he had a heart attack and died.

The original story was told by Jesus, and his summing up of this man's life was that he died a fool. He might have become an extremely rich man in the eyes of his contemporaries, but according to the measure by which Jesus judges a person's life he had missed something vital. Why? Because this man had spent all his life investing in things for this side of the grave but had neglected to invest in anything that would have eternal value. He had continually lived for the here and now and disregarded the hereafter. In living for himself, in seeing possessions as his god, in denying the reality of the life to come – he had never invested in the bank that determines how we shall live in that life.

Jesus was pointing to the spiritual reality that one of the events that follow death is a time of appraisal. It is a time when each of us will be asked to face up to how we have lived our life.

As in the case of the businessman, God will cast his eye over our lives and make his evaluation. An observation will be made on how we have responded to the spiritual as well as to the material. God will want to know much more about a person than how much they had in the bank.

In our culture, the idea of facing such a difficult and harsh assessment does not sit well. If there is anything difficult to be said in any appraisal, we prefer it to be in the context of hearing all the things we have done well. We can see that it's fine for evil people to be pulled up short and there and then be judged severely, but for *us* – well, we're not sure that's fair. So how does God arrive at a view of us?

It's not hard to see that if there is a God who cares about justice, then some kind of judgment in the next life is a possibility. Jesus does affirm that reality but curiously does not spend much time on the topic of judgment. The focus of Jesus is much more on how we can receive the forgiveness of God. His urgent message is not so much how we might avoid a judgment that would exclude us from the presence of God but how we might receive an experience of the love of God that will bind us to him, through death and into eternity.

When it comes to ideas about how we get to heaven, there is a huge diversity of opinion. Many focus on the idea of being a good person – of doing good deeds. Some look to religion as a guarantee of a heavenly future. But perhaps the largest response is a sense of trusting to luck. Surely God would not want to turn me away?

Some of the earliest church teaching says of Jesus that "he will come to judge the living and the dead". Christians believe that what we have said and done and thought (or *not*) will be held up in the pure light of the truth that is in Jesus, which will show it up for what it really is.

Jesus points us to a certain outcome. He suggests that those who genuinely desire to follow God can receive eternal life. He teaches that reconciliation between us and God was one of the most important reasons why he (Jesus) came to earth.

Getting to know and enjoy God for ever

Thirty years ago Stephen became a follower of Jesus. In reflecting on his life over those three decades his most precious memories have been those occasions when he has experienced or discovered something new about God. Having been brought up in a spiritual home, he had always believed that there was a God. When he was fourteen years of age someone explained to him that there was a difference between knowing about God and being in a place where he knew and experienced that reality in his daily life. The last thirty years have gradually revealed to him how absolutely wonderful and amazing God is.

Heaven will be a place where people enjoy the company of that amazing God for ever. No one will be able to say that they know all there is to know about God, but it will be a place where we can all experience more and more of who he is. If you have ever spent the evening in the company of a truly remarkable person – whether they be well known or not – you will know that such events can be absolutely wonderful experiences as you discover something about their life and their particular achievements. You end up sitting there mesmerized by their charisma; it doesn't matter what area they have excelled in – science, mathematics, or some act of heroism – you find yourself overwhelmed by the occasion.

But those experiences do not compare with the evenings that will be spent in eternity as we sit and eat and spend time with God. Could we ever get bored by spending time with God? Heaven will never be like the experience that David used to have. For over two years David received almost nightly calls from a person called Neville. Neville was one of life's more difficult cases. David imagined that having to talk to Neville all night was what hell must be like. If David was full of life when he picked up the phone to talk to Neville, he was in need of resuscitation by the end of the call. Neville would suck the life out of David.

That is not what it is going to be like as we live in heaven in the company of God. Because God is not a bit like Neville. He instead will keep us enthralled for ever – like a first love that never fades!

Conclusion

In the film *Indiana Jones and the Last Crusade*, the hero goes in search of the Holy Grail. This was the cup that Jesus supposedly drank out of at the Last Supper. What added to the impetus of the search was the belief that whoever drank from the cup would inherit immortality – eternal life. As you might expect, it was an amazing adventure getting there.

One of the reasons for the popularity of this film is that it expresses an appetite within us – a desire to touch the eternal, that which is immortal, to join oneself with the future. That's why people flock to see such films as *Star Wars*. There is an internal hunger to be joined with the eternal force. People dreamed of being the next Luke Skywalker, and of fulfilling their destiny.

In this chapter we have touched on what Jesus says is to be found in the future. The question that we may have to ask ourselves in the light of this is: Am I ready for that future? One of the points that Jesus often made when he taught the people of his day was the importance of being ready for their death. It was about ensuring that they knew where they were going when the time came for them to die, and about being certain of why they were so sure of their destination.

One day someone is going to write an obituary about you. What will they write? Will they speak of someone who approached death confidently, knowing what it was about and where they were going, or of someone terrified of death and unsure of their eternal home?

Chapter 4

How can I be happy?

Introduction

In recent years there has been a huge upsurge in publications, research, and debate about happiness. But what we mean by happiness is hard to pin down. What is happiness? Understandably, in our very consumer-driven society, happiness has come to be associated with wealth – material well-being. At its most basic, there is an assumption that the wealthier we are, the happier we should be.

In the film *The Pursuit of Happyness* we are introduced to Chris Gardner, an individual who decides to go on the search for a happy life. Disillusioned with his life as a seller of dental scanners, he becomes convinced that working as a stockbroker will give him the quality of life that he is looking for.

As Chris discovers, the pursuit of happiness is

not an easy one. The odds are stacked against him as only one in twenty of those who embark on this career qualify. As his journey unfolds, his wife decides to leave him because she is unwilling to struggle as he takes up this unsalaried opportunity. Life becomes even more difficult as he becomes homeless and he and his young son spend nights in public toilets or at shelters for the homeless.

Was the cost worth it? For Chris Gardner it seemed to be. As he is someone who interprets the American dream in materialistic terms, the film portrays him as getting there. He qualifies as a stockbroker and goes on to make considerable sums of money and live what he believes to be a deeply meaningful life.

Once we move beyond Hollywood, we discover that the connection between wealth and happiness is almost non-existent. Wealthy people are not necessarily happy people, and the less well-off are not necessarily miserable. But that does not mean that there is no connection between our material needs and the ability to be happy.

We do have basic needs: shelter, food, clothing, heat and light, to mention the obvious. But once we have achieved the elements we need in order to live at a modest level in the society in which we find ourselves, our level of happiness does not seem to increase as our wealth increases.

Our pursuit of happiness is so intense that so far, there have been over 336 million hits on the search engine Google for this word. With tens of thousands of books in print on this subject it seems that Aristotle was right when he claimed that happiness is "the ultimate goal of humanity". That much we can agree on. It's much harder to agree on how we reach that goal.

When we begin to reflect on the positive contribution that happiness makes to our lives, then it is no wonder that people have an innate desire to live well. Happiness is an extremely powerful commodity. Recent scientific research informs us that happy people live longer. Happy people tend to enjoy better mental health. Happy people are physically more resilient to illness. Happy people perform better in their chosen occupation and, it seems, have an all-round better quality of life.

In the happiness field, three connected questions assume importance. First, what is happiness? Second, what makes people happy? Third, when life is difficult, is it still possible to be happy? Accepting that life is tough for many people, we need to mull over whether there is a quality of happiness that can exist even during the worst of times.

What is happiness?

As we have noted, agreeing on a definition of happiness is not straightforward.

While at the gym recently, Paul was giving it his all on the cross-trainer when the person on the running machine next to him decided to initiate a conversation about where she had been on holiday recently and where she was going next. It was obvious that for her happiness was holiday-shaped. Being able to go on holiday as many times a year as possible, to exotic and different places, was her definition of what it means to be happy.

For others, happiness means the ideal life in the ideal home in the ideal location. For many, happiness is closely identified with the idea of pleasure. We can derive pleasure from a wide range of sources, such as hobbies and close family and personal relationships, as well as from enjoying the beauty of nature and the fascination of new experiences.

As we review the findings of modern research and the wisdom of the ancients, we discover that happiness is more a consequence than a purpose. Those who purely pursue happiness very rarely, if ever, find it. Happiness seems to come as a by-product of many other ingredients.

Perhaps this is no better illustrated than in the life of Solomon – reputably the wisest man who ever lived. Solomon records in his journal his attempts to discover a life worth living. Despite being the envy of many, this ancient king believed that there was more to life than what he had already experienced. So committed was he to this adventure that he could write that there was nothing he had not tried in his pursuit of the happy life. Solomon played the "What if" game. What if I have lots of money, will that make me happy? What if I own as much as anyone could own, would that make me happy? What if I taste as many of the experiences that it is possible to have in life, will that make me happy? By the end of his journal Solomon formulates what his search has taught him. His key conclusion is that a life worth living is not found through the pursuit of pleasure.

As well as encouraging us to see happiness as more a consequence than a purpose, the mystics of old and the researchers of today suggest that we perceive it as more a state of being than a momentary emotion. The father of positive psychology, Martin Seligman, proposes that happiness be read on a scale of -5 to +5. The closer to +5 you are, the happier you are. We shall explore next what might move us to that place. It is obvious that you can have spikes in life that raise your level, but what many people are searching for is a permanently higher level.

If we reflect on the observations made by those who have walked this earth in eons past, many comment that happiness is more about what is going on inside than about what is happening outwardly. There might be a momentary high caused by a significant rise in our salary or the purchase of some luxury goods, but after a very short period of time that diminishes. For happiness to stay around there needs to be an inner element.

Writing on the place of the soul, Dallas Willard likens it to a river that runs through the deeper parts of us. Happiness is found when that river is invigorated. For those who see themselves as spiritual beings as well as physical entities, happiness is about the interplay of our spirituality with our soul and body –

though we should not try to compartmentalize them. To be human is to be all of these.

Happiness relates to a quality of life. That quality is found through living out of a nourished soul. As relational beings we discover that happiness emerges as we experience meaningful relationships – the depth of our relationships increases as we tap into our inner reservoir.

Happy Gilmore is a film about someone who, having failed as a hockey player, decides to try his luck as a golfer. The cause of his career change is his attempt to pay off the large debt that his adorable grandmother has accrued. He is as good at golf as he was bad at hockey. Although unconventional in his attire, golf swing, and putting action, Gilmore becomes an instant hit on the tour. Despite a temper that often gets the better of him, this lovable rogue is presented to us as the archetypal happy guy.

Accepting that happiness is more a consequence than a purpose, more a state of being than a momentary emotion, more about what is going on inside than outwardly, and more about how you live, what is it that gives Gilmore (and us for that matter) the quality that we might describe as a happy life?

What makes people happy?

The 1970s television show *The Good Life* featured two couples, Tom and Barbara Good and Jerry and Margo Leadbetter. The plot was simple: when Tom reached his fortieth birthday he decided to retire from the rat race and go back to the land. What that meant was that he turned his back garden into his own personal smallholding and decided to live as much of a self-sufficient lifestyle as possible.

We were treated each week to the comical adventures of Tom and his wife as they tried to work through the difficulties that they had imposed on themselves by their commitment to the simple life. Along the way Jerry and Margo offered their comments on where their choices had got them. *The Good Life* explored whether Tom and Barbara's decision to go back to the land led to happiness.

Some research suggests that happiness is determined by where you live. The populations of some nations seem happier than others and, even within particular countries, populations in certain areas report greater or lesser degrees of happiness.

Some suggest that happiness can be enhanced by high levels of job satisfaction. It is not about the money you earn but the quality of your job – the extent to which the job you have fits well with the abilities you possess.

The writer and researcher Abraham Maslow reflected on the relationship between meeting our basic needs and finding life satisfaction. In 1943 he published a psychological theory that has become known as Maslow's hierarchy of needs. The hierarchy works like this:

Self-actualization
(Achieving individual potential)

Esteem
(Self-esteem and esteem from others)

Belonging
(Love, affection, being part of a group)

Safety
(Shelter, removal from danger)

Physiological
(Health, food, sleep)

Level one: Biological and physiological needs – air, food, drink, shelter, warmth, sex, sleep, etc.

Level two: Safety needs – protection from elements, security, order, law, limits, stability, etc.

Level three: Belonging and love needs – work group, family, affection, relationships, etc.

Level four: Esteem needs – self-esteem, achievement, mastery, independence, status, dominance, prestige, managerial responsibility, etc.

Level five: Self-actualization needs – realizing personal potential, self-fulfilment, seeking personal growth and peak experiences.

Only the first two levels can be purchased! Other research supports the work of Maslow, revealing that, beyond a certain point, neither money nor possessions make us happy – in fact quite the reverse. Why does the feel-good factor produced by new toys and more money desert us? Possessions ultimately disappoint, while good relationships have the capacity to take us to the higher levels of fulfilment, satisfaction, contentment, joy and happiness.

As expressed so insightfully by Oliver James in his popular book *Affluenza*, money is not the root of happiness or indeed the route to happiness. James called on the UK government to repent of its obsession with gross national product, leading people to believe that affluence solves all our problems.

So if money can buy us elements from only the first two levels of Maslow's hierarchy, practically speaking, how do we begin to attain the other levels of fulfilment? Research indicates three key areas. First, the ability to establish strong social networks. In the past those have usually been identified with good family networks, usually extending to grandparents, aunts, uncles, cousins, and beyond. Families were usually further strengthened by a good quality of local community – true "neighbourhoods" where people really did look out for one another.

Second, the ability to perceive that one's life has meaning. To some extent, in the past, meaning was easily located in the strong networks of identity found within the extended family. In such a situation we matter to others, we are known and we can know other people. But meaning in life goes beyond such personal relationships. In the past, religious faith helped to provide frameworks of meaning but, whether we are "religious" people or not, we do need to derive some meaning from an understanding of how we connect in some meaningful way, through our work, our abilities, and what we give to others.

Third, happiness or life satisfaction is also related to our ability to set goals in life. This does not just mean work-related goals, either. Some research suggests that those who are the most happy in their retirement have established some clear goals for their post-employment stage of life.

These three key areas need some further development for us to be able to see how they work out in practice.

Time magazine published an article at the beginning of 2005 summarizing the findings of psychologists in the area of happiness. They identified what they called "eight secrets of happiness"[8]: count your blessings, savour life's joys, practise acts of kindness, invest in friends, learn to forgive, thank a mentor, take care of your body and soul, and develop a strategy to help you cope with stress and difficult situations.

As we integrate these various disciplines into the rhythm of life, most of us will improve our personal level of happiness. The research considered in *Time*

---

8   See our book *The 8 Secrets of Happiness*, Oxford: Lion Hudson, 2009.

magazine includes aspects of spirituality – deeper values that require some further reflection. In reality it is very hard to integrate the advice contained in the *Time* survey without being aware of the spiritual dimension of who we are.

For example, it is hard to thank others, learn to forgive or invest in friends without a deep commitment to the idea that others have an intrinsic value. In some profound sense, life itself is sacred; as human beings we have an intrinsic worth. In the teaching of Jesus these ideas are themselves dependent on the conviction that we are made in the image of God and that we find our true selves when our lives reflect that image which stands at the core of our being. Happiness is in some way connected to becoming all that we were created to be in terms of our gifts, our ethical life and our spiritual development.

For a few years now, the BBC website has been hosting some pages on the science of happiness. They ask the question, "Is there a formula for happiness?" There is a strong case that happiness equals knowing how to live well. That involves becoming the person you were created to be. It is about living out of your divine DNA.

A little while ago David and his family spent several hours searching for his car keys. He was going out to buy some food and he couldn't find his keys. Convinced that he had put them down somewhere in the lounge but unable to find them, he encouraged all the other members of the household to help him. Adamant that the keys were somewhere in the lounge (or maybe the kitchen), he refused to allow anyone to look elsewhere. Finally, after looking in every conceivable location, his wife decided to go and check the pockets of his coat, which was hanging up in the cupboard. Just like David, when it comes to finding happiness many of us might be looking in the wrong place. In seeing ourselves as people made in the image of God, we begin to get an idea of where we could be looking to discover the happiness we seek.

When life is difficult, is it still possible to be happy?

In his 1978 bestseller *The Road Less Traveled*, author M. Scott Peck notes that life is difficult. So, is it possible to be happy even during life's most difficult moments?

When Jane was eighteen she was diagnosed with ME. For the last twenty years she has lived with ME and it has been a debilitating disease for her. It has affected her university education and her ability to work and live an independent life, and yet, when you meet her and talk to her, you find somebody who is truly happy. This is not someone who puts on a superficial smile for the sake of those who cross her path or someone who is trying to smile despite what she is living with. Here is a woman who in the middle of those very difficult circumstances has some sort of paradise in her heart that she draws on and which enables her to live well with ME.

If you were to talk to her she would tell you that this happiness comes from the hope that she has. Jane has attempted to dig deep into her inner resources, to draw upon her intrinsic spirituality. She is aware of her value as a person. She is not defined by her ME but by her value as someone who reflects the image of God in ever-growing ways. Does she cry sometimes? Absolutely. Does she get frustrated sometimes? Certainly. But in the midst of those difficult situations there is something hopeful in her heart.

Research has shown that those who have good

coping mechanisms often handle life's difficult moments better than those who don't. For some of us, these mechanisms will include time spent talking to or being with friends. For others, they may mean preparing in advance for what you know is coming or, when it hits, being able to take time out of your busy life to replenish your resources.

Running alongside establishing good coping mechanisms or strategies is the habit of nurturing a world view that is consistent with being spiritual people in a material world. Perhaps in no other area does the input of spirituality contain more value than in how it helps us deal with the sadness of life. As we have already illustrated, the presence of faith helped Jane to understand the value of her personal challenge for herself. It transformed her view of suffering.

Closely connected with the arrival of a fresh perspective on suffering is the presence of hope. When your view of life is changed, it opens the door for a change in what you understand follows life – how you see your eternity. For Jane, her understanding of life is that death is not the end; therefore, what goes on in this world should be interpreted in the light of what happens after death.

As we have already indicated, this opened up for Jane the possibility of seeing suffering as a place of betterment, but what it also did was bring the realization that the hardships that this life throws at us do not go on for ever. There will be a time when Jane no longer has ME. Ultimately there will be a bright tomorrow, a time when she will not run out of energy, when she will not have to stay in bed today because she got overtired yesterday. Jane lives her present life to the full in the belief that life on this planet is not the whole story.

Lastly, what helps us cope with life's difficult times is the realization that God is with us as we go through them. Perhaps this is no better visualized than in the well-known poem "Footsteps in the Sand", which paints the picture of how during life's most trying moments there is only one set of footprints in the sand and not two. The reason being that God carries us during life's tragic events.

A friend of ours has just failed to conceive after IVF treatment. It was her last chance and she is emotionally devastated. She faces a complete reimagining of her future. Ever since she was a child she has dreamed of being a mum, and throughout her married life she has worked with children with the hope of one day stopping work to bring up her own. In the middle of all these tears (and there are a lot of tears) and the pain (and there is a lot of pain), if you stare into her eyes, you see something – a sparkle, a glimmer – that will ensure that she does not stay where she is but will move on to become once again somebody who is happy.

Will this happy aura return quickly and easily? Probably not. There will be moments when it will be lost through the reopening of this deep wound. But as she attempts to live her life as someone who is infinitely and intrinsically valuable, someone made in the image of God, there is for her the hope of living a meaningful life. Life can indeed be difficult, but there are resources that enable us to overcome the heartaches.

Conclusion

When somebody pulls out their camera you often hear the instruction "Smile, everybody; smile". Although happy to put on a smile for the camera, if we are honest there are moments, even seasons, when many of us struggle to smile, because life is incredibly burdensome and difficult. What we have been looking at in this chapter are some of the sources that will bring happiness to all of us a form of happiness that is not dependent on circumstances but which has a depth to it such that, even though we find ourselves in the most difficult of situations, it will still enable us to have an inner joy. That source is spiritual and is connected with living out our lives as we were created to live them.

Chapter 5

Why is there suffering in the world?

Introduction

David was in his early sixties and wanted to talk about something that had had a huge impact on his whole life. Eighteen months earlier David's wife, Maureen, had died, and he needed to talk it through.

Maureen had been feeling tired but had thought nothing of it. Life was busy for this retired couple, and after a particularly hectic time of looking after their grandchildren she had thought that it was nothing more than overdoing it a little. When the tiredness failed to go away she went to the doctor expecting him to tell her to take it easy and to give her a tonic. To be on the safe side the doctor suggested that they should conduct some routine tests. Those tests flagged up that there might be something more sinister going on – it turned out to be an aggressive form of cancer. Seven weeks after the first set of tests she died.

With tears in his eyes, David talked about how he had lost the love of his life. They had been together for over forty years. But now she was gone. He was devastated. He talked about the fact that he had considered suicide, and if it wasn't for his daughter he would have taken his own life. For him there was no point left in life, and so he had lost the desire to live.

He wanted to know why it had happened as it had. She was a good woman, and as a couple they had always tried to help people. His wife was a wonderful person – why did she have to die so relatively young, and so quickly?

It isn't hard to see that life can sometimes seem very unfair. We only have to look at some of the nursery rhymes we were taught as a child to realize that all is not good in our world.

Some research was undertaken recently on the things that people are most concerned about. Many of those questioned spoke about the personal suffering that they or a close family member had experienced. Others told of their worries about national problems that were affecting their local communities. There were some who noted their fear of the impact that global issues such as the environment were having and would have on their lives and the lives of their children.

What underlies all these concerns is an acknowledgment that things are not quite right in our world. The underlying question is: Why? Why do bad things happen, not only to good people, but why do they happen at all? Why do they happen in remote parts of the world, unknown to us except through the news media; why do they happen to those we know, and, most of all, why do they happen to *us*? Even if we have not yet experienced a particularly serious difficulty, we know that we might, even if we choose not to think about it.

People want to know why there are problems on their streets. Why can't they go out safely at night in some areas? Then there are those who want to know why society is breaking down and why there are such global problems as poverty, AIDS, and environmental degradation.

When it comes to looking at why there is so much suffering in the world we are obviously dealing with a very complex set of problems. In this chapter we will consider several paths that offer us an explanation of why there might be suffering in the world. At the same time we acknowledge that this question is far more complex than simply understanding these various routes.

Obviously, in looking at this important question, we are dealing with a deeply emotional life issue. For many there is enormous personal heartache involved. Our aim is to be both sympathetic and honest in our consideration of why there is so much pain and difficulty in our world. We hope we will strike the right balance, but where we fail, it is not because we are intentionally trying to deny either the issues or the pain.

And the last comment to be made as we explore what C. S. Lewis called "the problem of pain" is that we are not dealing with an issue that has anything to do with fairness. Many of us have seen how good things happen to bad people and how really bad things happen to good people. Quite often there is no obvious rhyme or reason for why that should be.

So then, where are some of the places that we should think of journeying to in order to get a better understanding of why there is so much suffering in our world?

Our own thoughts and actions

Perhaps the reason for the suffering in the world is due to what goes on in our own lives.

Magnum ice creams recently ran a creative advertising campaign based on the seven deadly sins – those sins that the earliest followers of Jesus deemed to be particularly harmful and destructive to a healthy lifestyle: jealousy, vanity, lust, gluttony, sloth, greed, and envy. The company named some of their ice-cream products after these sins and then encouraged us to enjoy them.

As we look into the centre of our being we find that many of these vices are to be found there. Unfortunately, our enjoyment of them has far more serious consequences than just putting on a few pounds of fat.

Mary's story is the tragic tale of a life ruined by debt. Mary was always buying stuff. Pretty soon she had spent all her own money and was borrowing from friends and family. When someone noticed what was going on and challenged her about her spending habits, she was quick to deny any problem, citing the need to get these things for herself or for her family. When it got to the point where no one would lend her money, she turned to theft and finally to loan agencies that charged interest rates that put her deeper into debt month by month.

Some difficulties arise from our own personal apathy. We all know that there are some major environmental challenges facing the world and yet so few of us do anything to help deal with the problems. We cover up our lack of effort with the excuses of "But what can *I* do?" or "The real problem is these large manufacturers". It is fair to say that the contribution we can make is minuscule in comparison with the enormity of the problem and that there are more significant culprits who do need to pull their weight, but when apathy rules and good people do nothing, the situation becomes significantly worse.

When good people do nothing then whole neighbourhoods can be destroyed by the few vandals who live there. When good people do nothing then those in authority who have a warped sense of what is right and wrong can implement projects and schemes that damage the less fortunate and the vulnerable. When good people do nothing then society can be infiltrated and ransacked by those who have ulterior agendas.

Some social commentators have begun to identify

the emergence of a "blame culture". When something goes wrong, when something tragic happens or even when an accident occurs, we all demand to know who is to blame.

We need to consider, painful as it is, whether there are occasions when the reason that bad things are happening in our own lives or in the lives of others is due to our own actions. Are we encouraging forced labour in some countries of the world because of our craving for certain foods or clothing? Do we encourage sweatshops because we are prepared to pay only a certain amount of money for our goods?

King Solomon once noted that one of the great truths about life is that evil and insanity reside in the human heart. Does Solomon, renowned for his wisdom, have a point?

The behaviour of others

A whole family were left devastated recently by the discovery that the man of the house had been having an affair for the last four years. Bored with his lot in life and wanting a little more excitement, he had got involved with one of the women who attended the same club as him. She had recently been divorced and liked the attention. Very quickly their enjoyment of each other's company turned physical.

This man's double life was exposed when the woman he had been having the affair with decided to let his wife know. To say the least, the fallout from his actions has been painful and widespread. As he was a significant figure in his community, the national press decided to pick up on the story. It was covered over several weeks in different papers. His wife, overwhelmed by the betrayal, had an emotional breakdown. Their children are in shock.

As we have already noted above, Solomon believed that evil and insanity reside in the human heart. What he went on to say was that unfortunately, through no fault of your own, like those who are knocked down and killed by reckless drivers, you can become a victim of other people's evil and insanity.

As fish are caught in a cruel net,
or birds are taken in a snare,
so people are trapped by evil times
that fall unexpectedly upon them.

Ecclesiastes 9:12, TNIV

In many senses, this is what happened to that particular family. Unable to deal with the routine boredom of life, this man risked losing and then damaging his family. In losing such a gamble no one knows if they will ever recover.

When Ron's son Stuart passed his driving test, one of the attitudes that Ron was keen to enforce on his son was both to watch his own driving and also to keep an eye on how other people were handling their cars. As a policeman, Ron had seen far too many tragedies where an innocent person had been badly injured or killed because of the reckless way that another person had driven. Keen to help his son stay safe, he was eager to impress on him the need to always watch how others were handling the road as well as to drive safely himself. This attitude is something that all of us want to instil in our own children. It doesn't matter how careful *you* are; it is still possible to be the victim of other people's stupidity.

There was a tragic story in the British media recently about a teenager who was beaten and killed by a couple of local lads just for the fun of it. The boy concerned had been out for the night and had decided to walk home rather than hail a taxi. It was a lovely night; it had been a fun evening out, so what a great way to round it off by walking home along the coastal path.

Unknown to this young man, two lads, bored with their evening and looking for a bit of amusement, had decided to pounce on him and beat him up. They ended up killing him. He lost his promising young life because of the actions of others.

Whatever you think of the Ten Commandments, one of the benefits of having such a code of practice is that it gives us a framework for living, which should protect us and others from the evil that resides in the human heart.

Why is there suffering in the world? One cause is that sometimes other people act recklessly or selfishly or with evil intent, and others are harmed because of it.

Attitudes and outcomes

When the Smith family moved into their new home they were warmly welcomed by their neighbours. It had been a long time since a youngish family had lived in that part of the town, and people were delighted to see new faces. Then it was discovered that the reason why the father was absent from the family home was that he was serving a two-year sentence in a local prison for burglary. Those who had initially welcomed the family cooled in their manner towards them.

Unfortunately for the Smith family, some of those who found out about their difficult and vulnerable situation decided to take it upon themselves to ensure that the whole family and not just the husband suffered for his crimes. Over the following months they had stones thrown at their home, they were jeered at when they walked down the street, the kids were picked on at school, and rubbish was regularly thrown into their garden.

Justice had clearly been served in that the husband had been caught, tried, and sentenced. What the rest of the family had to endure was clearly unfair. But then that is one of the reasons why there is suffering in the world: any group of people can set themselves up as having the right to be judge and jury. They might feel that they have the right, but in reality they do not.

These collective attitudes and actions, whether owned by the majority or by a vocal minority, have caused many people throughout history to suffer.

One of the other reasons why some people

experience suffering is that they are devalued by others. Countless numbers of African families were torn apart by the selfishness and greed of others. Seeing these fellow human beings as of lesser value than themselves, slave traders thought nothing of treating them as subhuman, herding them like cattle into small pens and shipping them around the world to work as slaves to all who could afford them. The fact that a large number died in transit was not something that concerned slave traders too much. William Wilberforce, whom we mentioned earlier, made it his life's work to see slavery abolished.

Today, people are still treated as cheap commodities by others. Vulnerable women are trafficked. Young children are sold to factory owners because their families cannot feed them.

In our first chapter, where we offered a different way of seeing ourselves, the sum of what we were suggesting was that each of us might begin to see others (as well as ourselves) as the priceless beings that they are. When any society fails to appreciate the worth of any of its citizens, then that society inevitably generates human misery.

Other attitudes are equally harmful. How many

people have become the victim of a company's greed? How often do you hear the suggestion that a company has decided that it has made enough profit and therefore will not be making anyone redundant? You sometimes get the idea that greed, in the shape of the profit motive, is a noble ideal to aspire to.

Our greed has obviously had a serious impact on the environment and our use of natural resources. How much damage have we inflicted on the natural world because of our pursuit of passing desires, elevated by effective media advertising into basic needs or even rights?

Another problem arises from our elevation of the individual above and beyond the good of the community. We do need to look after the individual, to make sure that they have rights and that their rights are honoured. However, when individualism becomes a byword for selfishness, then something has gone wrong. Alongside our commitment to the individual, it is important to acknowledge the role of the community and our responsibilities to one another. Looking out for others is something that should transcend colour, class, geography, political allegiance, and religious affiliation.

Our relationship with God

The teaching of Jesus offers us a perspective on the underlying issues that contribute to suffering in the world. This could be referred to as the deeper story.

According to the New Testament, an important cause of suffering is the fracturing of relationships between human beings, between humanity and the created order, and ultimately between humankind and God.

Supposedly, in eons past, our ancestors had a very happy relationship with God. All was good in the garden. The image painted is one of our being friends with God and enjoying all the good things that he brought into that relationship – joy, peace, health and life. We walked with God, and everything worked together for good.

That perspective is presented in a series of stories – the garden of Eden, the life of the earliest humans – which highlight the essential waywardness of the human mind. The stories suggest that we have an innate tendency to seek after things and experiences that are not good for us, and to ignore our true destiny and purpose.

Those same stories recount that God has never

been content with this state of affairs, and constantly seeks to draw us back to healthy human relationships and a fulfilling relationship with him. The role of Jesus in God's desire to bring reconciliation to humanity is a hugely important story which needs to be explored in more detail elsewhere.

Natural disasters

In offering an explanation for why there is suffering in the world, it quickly becomes apparent that there are several supplementary questions. On the face of it, some suffering does not flow from human action but rather from natural disasters. Whether they be earthquake, hurricane, fire or tempest, there does not seem to be a human moral ingredient in such events. Why is the world constructed in such a way that natural disasters occur? Those who believe that there is an all-powerful and good God inevitably have to ask why he would allow such things to happen.

Charles Darwin developed some serious questions about the relationship of God to the created order. Those questions did not begin with his study of evolution on the Galapagos Islands, but rather on his way to that destination. While travelling to those islands, he and the ship's company witnessed a huge and destructive earthquake in Chile. The impact of that event had a profound effect on the young Darwin's mind.

But even in the case of what seems to be a purely natural disaster, we can begin to see that moral issues are not entirely absent. For example, in recent times we have been able to observe the consequences of another serious earthquake in Chile and one in Haiti. Despite the fact that the earthquake in Chile was far more powerful than the one in Haiti, fewer than 1,000 people lost their lives in the Chilean earthquake, while possibly 300,000 died in Haiti. Why was this?

A key reason was the different construction of the buildings. A choice had been made in Chile to build to the highest standards of anti-earthquake technology. In poor, badly administered Haiti, with all the complexities that surround such circumstances, some would argue that there was no will or means to invest in earthquake-resistant buildings, resulting in devastating consequences.

The core (and difficult) argument of the Bible in relation to good, evil, and suffering suggests that the world we live in is fractured in a number of ways and that we cannot place human morality in an isolated box. Ultimately, all that takes place in the world has a deep inner relationship, so complex that we cannot unravel all of the paths and patterns.

The Bible also makes it clear that God takes responsibility for both good and evil. It is not that he is the instigator of evil – far from it – but the fact that he is both all-powerful and the ongoing creator of the world means that he allows evil to take place. In that sense he is the author of both light and dark, of ecstatic joy and profound sadness. By allowing the possibility of evil and suffering, God takes ultimate responsibility for its existence and reality. Why has God made the world in such a way? In one sense it is vital that we have contrasts in life. We cannot live for ever on mountain-top experiences. But that is not sufficient to answer the cry of those who suffer extreme physical pain or experience the heartbreak of the terrible loss of loved ones.

There are some questions that we cannot fully know the answer to in the sense of a complete and tidy explanation. In these areas it is sometimes helpful to apprehend rather than comprehend. In other words, we can begin to sense where the answer might lie, rather than fully understanding the detail of what an answer might be. That sense of apprehending a deeper answer is found in the works of writers such as C. S. Lewis, in his well-known "Narnia" series. In *The Last Battle*, Lewis conveys the idea that this present world is a shadow (or the *Shadowlands*, as the book and film about the story of Lewis's life is called) of a world that is yet to come. That does not mean that this world is simply a rehearsal for a future world. This present reality matters precisely because it is infused with and invaded by elements of the world to come. We cannot fully know that future world, but it involves a fuller encounter with God. That same God is involved in the here and now of our everyday lives.

So where is God?

This leads us to a slightly different set of questions. Does God care when we suffer, or does he just look on? Where is God in the midst of suffering? What is the point of believing in God? Can God make any difference in a suffering world?

It does not take much imagination to see that it hardly makes sense for God to continually interfere in the world in the way that superheroes do – a kind of cosmic Superman always ensuring that no harm comes to us, regardless of our moral choices. But that does not mean that God does not intervene. Those who believe in God pray for intervention and would claim that they do see answers to prayer, especially but not exclusively in the area of healing.

God's involvement in this world is far more complex and subtle than the Superman approach! Even when someone is healed, apparently miraculously, of a serious illness, it does not guarantee that they will not get ill again, have a tragic accident, die young or suffer pain. Ultimately they will die from some cause, even if it is just old age.

We believe, as Christians, that God sent Jesus to this earth, and this gives us a different perspective on suffering.

First, suffering can have a redemptive, moral purpose. The experience of personal suffering can cause people to cry out to God. A difficult period in their life may make them aware of God, and more responsive to him. For others, suffering can have a purifying or transforming effect. The presence of hardship has reshaped attitudes and behaviour patterns that they had struggled to change.

Second, many of those who have experienced suffering have indicated that God was very much present with them in their darkest moments. As we have already mentioned, God does not deliberately cause us to suffer, though we can certainly see that on occasion he allows suffering. In that suffering, it is possible to experience God as accompanying us through it. He is himself the suffering God, the crucified God. He is present not in the sense of a spectator but as someone who wants to accompany us through the darkness.

In our opening story, we described how David was devastated by losing his wife Maureen. When Paul met David, listening to his pain and hearing his heartbreak, he picked up that David was also aware that God was present with him in his darkest moments. The death of his wife did not make sense, and it was not fair, but he knew he was not alone.

Suffering, pain, disease, and ultimately death can be tragic and even too difficult to talk about on occasion, but suffering does not have to be the last word in our lives. Some years ago Martin met a young woman called Suzanne. She had a debilitating disease of the spine which would kill her before she reached old age. In many cases, people with this condition die before they reach adulthood. Her single mother had struggled to give her a childhood worth living. It was a tough story.

As Martin came to know Suzanne, he was struck by her ability to live her life to its fullest potential. Against the odds she reached adulthood, went to university, and obtained a job as a social worker. She was always wheelchair-dependent and struggled with many basic movements, but she always insisted on one thing, which Martin heard her express in open prayer: "God, I thank you that I am alive."

The sentiment that comes from Suzanne's heartfelt prayer can help us to turn suffering towards a good outcome.

Chapter 6

What is the spiritual world and how does it impact my life?

Introduction

Have you ever asked yourself whether there is more to life than what you can see, touch or comprehend? The possibility of a spiritual dimension to life features significantly in recent cinema productions. A long list of Hollywood blockbusters explore what life would be like if there were angels or ghosts or vampires.

Then there are films like *Next*, starring Nicolas Cage, which explores what life would be like for those who have supernatural abilities. The storyline features someone who keeps getting premonitions of what lies ahead. These premonitions enable him to escape harm and to live well. These abilities also make him an attractive form of defence for the FBI against terrorists. Such premonitions are widely documented. Do they come from a world that we cannot see, or are they expressions of a higher form of human life – or simply the result of too much cheese for supper the night before?

Many people today pray. When our prayers are answered positively, should we see this as just coincidence or wishful thinking? Or are such outcomes evidence of a world that cannot be seen?

In the film *Contact*, starring Jodie Foster, we are introduced to an astronomer who has an out-of-this-world experience, so mind-blowing that it changes for ever how she will see the world in which she lives. She begins her journey as a scientist whose understanding of the universe is determined by what her hands, eyes, and mind tell her is reality. Her grasp of what is out there has been formed by the scholarly books she has read, the numerous experiments she has conducted, and the hours she has spent staring out into space through the many giant telescopes she has worked with.

And then she goes on a space flight that changes everything. The flight lasts only forty seconds, but for her it feels like hours. On her journey she travels to a world that is beyond her imagination, a mystical world that is overwhelmingly beautiful, a new dimension in which she is able to spend some time with the spirit of her father.

As a result of this mystical journey, her understanding of the universe is expanded and transformed. For Foster's character there is now a mystical or spiritual element to life that is as real as the physical one she lives in. Today, many people hold a similar perspective on reality to that of Foster's character after her out-of-body experience. They have concluded that there is a spiritual reality as well as a physical one.

There must be as many different takes on reality as there are people. Humanity is for ever asking the question, "What if?" and coming up with a myriad of different answers.

Graham, a high-school teacher, took a flight to the Caribbean for a well-earned holiday. Friends who enjoyed discussing the spiritual world had got him asking himself, "What if? What if it's really true?" But when he came home, he told his colleagues and students that he had flown in the clouds of heaven but seen no sign of God. God was a figment of our imagination: wishful thinking.

Maybe Graham didn't fly high enough! The astronaut Edgar Mitchell, who participated in the Apollo 14 moon flight, experienced life-changing insights that could almost be likened to a vision on his way home from space. As he looked at Planet Earth, a fragile little blue sphere suspended there, the only one like it, home of all his hopes and dreams, his loves and fears, he had a sudden overwhelming sense of the interconnectedness of all life: that all of existence – everything – is joined together in one great web of life and meaning, part of a process both intelligent and aware. This was not a passing emotion; it proved to be profoundly transformative, changing the course of the rest of his life. Edgar Mitchell had woken up to the spiritual realm.

All around the world, many people who might not describe themselves as adherents to a mainstream religion nonetheless are intrigued by psychic fairs or daily newspaper horoscopes or TV dramas exploring the possibility of alien intelligence. The sales of angel cards, healing crystals, and meditation tapes all point to the magnetism of mystery for the human mind. There is something in the human spirit that says, "There must be more to life than this."

"May the Force be with you." What Force?

In the most recent UK census, 390,000 people entered "Jedi Knight" as their chosen religion; so many that the census officials allocated Jedi Knight a code of its own and included it on their list of officially recognized religions.

The Star Wars movies have captured the imagination of thousands. You can even get a ringtone that announces an incoming text message with an alert in Yoda's voice: "A message from the Dark Side there is."

The Force, an energy that permeates the whole galaxy, is something that you cannot touch with physical hands, see with your eyes, taste with your tongue, or smell or hear. Yet it manifests in the physical realm as the Jedi Knights tap into its power, harnessing it in their struggle against the evil Empire. "Use the Force, Luke!" Yoda urges his Jedi student – "Use the Force!"

The Force is benevolent, but it has a Dark Side – some characters have wrongly channelled its energy to corrupt and selfish ends, to dominate and oppress others, and to impose the egotistical agenda against which the Rebel Alliance so heroically fights back.

Is it a game – just a story, just a movie? Or is there really a mystical force beyond and behind the physical world and interacting with it? Are there really forces of light and darkness – good and evil – locked in combat? Is there truly and actually a choice to be made – an issue about whose side we align ourselves with?

Epics like the Lord of the Rings and Star Wars film series exercise a powerful and transformative hold on our imagination. But is it simply the power of a good story, or is there a meta-narrative – an overarching reality interweaving with our lives and determining our destiny?

The last experiment

As we think about whether the spiritual exists or not, we also need to take into account the experiences of countless thousands of people who claim to have had an encounter with the "other" and for whom it has been a profound experience, bringing hope, balance and even deep integration to their lives. That sense of the "other" spans from beauty and awe to an awareness of the power of love.

In his 1948 book *Love Can Open Prison Doors*,

Starr Daily, a hardened criminal from the 1930s who had an unexpected, direct, life-changing spiritual experience alone in his prison cell, said this:

> *I am telling you about a power that resides in the hearts of men, which is a power greater than any power ever to be discovered in the realm of natural science. It is a power possessed by all, but recognized by few. It is the most dynamic and readily accessible power in the universe of men.*

Starr Daily said that the power is love, and comes from God:

> *I call love the last experiment, because though it is the closest and most fundamental thing in a person's life, it is the last thing he will turn to for help when he is in distress. In talking to you about love I shall not get mushy and sentimental. For love is everything that sentimentalism is not. Love is power, while sentimentalism is the misuse of power. In its practical application love is as precise and scientific as mathematics. Without it there could be no universe, no cell organization of any kind. Because love is the only integrating power in existence. It is all that can establish order out of chaos or maintain order in chaos.*

He goes on to say: "Love is God in action."

Maslow saw it

The sense of the spiritual, an awareness of beauty, a sensitivity to love, has also been part of the work of some psychologists. As we saw in chapter 4, in the 1940s an American psychologist, Abraham Maslow, developed the concept of a "hierarchy of human needs". He formulated the proposition that each of us has five levels of basic need, hierarchical in the sense that only when the first has been satisfied can a person feel the second, only when that is satisfied can he feel the third, and so on. It is these needs that drive us through life.

At the top of Maslow's triangle (see chapter 4) comes self-actualization. This complex term includes the need for creativity and spontaneity, for morality and freedom from prejudice, for problem-solving and the acceptance of reality – aspects of life related to identity and purpose. Towards the end of his life, Maslow suggested an additional level that he called "self-transcendence". At this level, qualities that can only be called spiritual begin to become important:

humility, a sense of responsibility and compassion for the plight of others, altruism of outlook.

Maslow's self-transcendence seems to be embarking on Starr Daily's last experiment of love.

Our primary need

Maslow's hierarchy of needs proposes that we are not able to pay attention to our mental and spiritual level of needs until our basic physical and emotional needs have been satisfied. If you push a man's head under water and hold it there, he won't be wondering about techniques of meditation, he'll be focusing entirely on AIR! Because we pay attention to things in that order – our physical needs first, our spiritual needs last – we can make the mistake of thinking that it is a hierarchy of importance as well as a hierarchy of need: that our physical needs are more important than our mental needs; and our spiritual needs are a kind of add-on, a hobby to do in the evenings when the real work of the day is done (and not every evening but only in the ones that are left over when we've attended to the essentials like digging the garden or going to the gym).

The Bible opens with the words "In the beginning

God..." and that is of itself a profound observation about the nature of things – that they start with spirit and work outwards creatively to the physical realm. In the beginning God created the heavens and the earth: an assertion that matter comes from spirit, relies on spirit, is spiritual in origin.

There is a difference between "primary" and "basic". Our basic needs and realities may be physical, while our primary needs and realities are spiritual. Indeed, we say that a person is reduced to a "vegetable" when their body is alive – breathing, sleeping, waking, eating, excreting – but there is no sign of cognitive processes remaining. And our hope for a person in that condition is that one day they will again express ideas, relationship, love and friendship – those things that belong to the spiritual realm of life.

What happens when we are disconnected from the divine?

Rabbi Hugo Gryn was imprisoned in Auschwitz by the Nazis at the age of thirteen, along with his father, mother and younger brother. They had made escape plans when the situation worsened in Germany, but in the end abandoned those plans because they could not bear to leave the grandparents behind.

Hugo's mother and brother died in the concentration camp, but he and his father survived. In his adult life as a rabbi, Hugo used to tell of an occasion when, in the camp one day, he had come upon his father lighting a little lamp. For oil, he was using the scrapings of margarine he had been given, which he had saved up for this purpose. Hugo remonstrated with his father. They had so little to eat; they needed every morsel they could get. What was he thinking of, to waste his margarine like that? Hugo's father explained that today was Chanukkah, the Jewish festival of light, and he had saved the margarine so that on that holy day he would be able to observe the customs of the festival. He told his son: "You and I had to go once for over a week without proper food and another time almost three days without water, but you cannot live for three minutes without hope."

In his book *Chasing Shadows*, Rabbi Hugo Gryn wrote: "No one is safe when religious or ethnic prejudice is tolerated, when racism is rife and when decent, well-meaning people keep quiet because it is prudent."[9] He

9   London: Penguin Books, 2001.

is right, of course, and this assertion has implications for Maslow's hierarchy of needs: it is evidence that unless we pay attention to the spiritual needs at the top of the triangle – morality, kindness, goodness – we make ourselves vulnerable to forces that threaten us at more basic levels of the triangle – stability of society, safety, provision of shelter and food. People in moral and spiritual health will look after the physical needs (provided the physical resources exist) of the weakest as well as the strong: people in physical health will not necessarily look after the moral and spiritual needs of anybody, even themselves!

It makes sense if you think about it. People who prioritize goodness, kindness, generosity, mercy, sharing, honesty, peace, justice, and self-discipline are going immediately to address many of the problems that challenge our everyday well-being: war, inequality, crime, oppression, cruelty, greed.

So hooking up with the Force, tuning into the spiritual realm, offers us the potential to improve not only our personal well-being but that of our whole society, and what happens in the whole of society will in turn loop back to affect us again, because "society" inevitably includes us too.

A transforming encounter

An awareness of the spiritual realm puts us in touch with power for transformation – with the possibility of becoming the people we were meant to be. It becomes increasingly possible to overcome the habits that disappoint us and which hurt others while, at the same time, developing those qualities that we so admire in others.

The Bible tells the story of King David, whose reign was a golden era for the people of ancient Israel. A warrior king, passionate and red-blooded, David went through some hard times in the course of his life, some of them of his own making. But the Bible describes King David as "a man after God's own heart"; he was hooked up to the Force, tuned into Spirit.

Among other things, King David was a musician: the book of Psalms in the Bible was his songbook. Psalm 23 is by David:

The Lord is my shepherd, I shall not be in want.
He makes me lie down in green pastures,
He leads me beside quiet waters,
He restores my soul.

He guides me in paths of righteousness for his name's sake.
Even though I walk through the valley of the shadow of death,
I will fear no evil,
For you are with me;
Your rod and your staff, they comfort me.

You prepare a table before me in the presence of my enemies.
You anoint my head with oil; my cup overflows.
Surely goodness and love will follow me all the days of my life,
And I will dwell in the house of the Lord for ever.

In his boyhood, David was a shepherd. The "rod and staff" that he mentions in the song are tools used like a shepherd's crook, to guide, rescue, and defend the sheep. They are not meant for beating us!

So David compared his experience of tapping into the spiritual realm to a sheep travelling through life with a shepherd he could trust to take care of him, watch over him when he was vulnerable, provide for his needs, rescue him when he got lost, and defend him from attack. Again and again the Bible comes back to this picture of living in the spiritual realm. It's an image of the Force not as something like electricity or gas or water, impersonal but all around us, but as a Person, who watches over us and travels with us; someone who cares about us, whom we can trust to be our friend.

When Starr Daily wrote about "the last experiment", making contact with a power so amazing it can turn our lives upside down, he was thinking of people reaching out to make a connection with a loving God.

The proposition we are working with here is that the spiritual power so many have discovered is actually personal – Someone, not something. As we outlined in chapter 2, God in the Christian tradition is someone who is loving, just, faithful, jealous, and creative.

Taste and see – how do you engage with the spiritual?

But even if your name is Harry Potter and you have a mysterious scar on your forehead identifying you as The One, you still need to take some time to learn how to handle your broom in a game of Quidditch and find out how to approach a hippogriff without getting attacked.

The spiritual realm is all around us, and we are spiritual creatures by our own nature; we are already in it. But understanding our spiritual nature, and learning how to bring that potential through into our everyday lives, takes time and thought and discipline. It's fun, but it helps to know what you're doing.

Writing on the spiritual disciplines available to us, spiritual guru Dallas Willard categorizes them into two primary groups. There are disciplines that help to create space to meet with God, and disciplines that help to push out of our lives things that might get in the way of meeting God.

You can experiment with different disciplines before you settle on those that best work for you. Don't think that just because such a discipline worked for your friend, it will necessarily also be the best one for you. We are all different and therefore need to discover the spiritual workout pattern that suits us best.

One summer day, when Suzy was a little girl, she went through the kitchen on her way to play out in the garden. She stopped by the kitchen table, where her mum was sitting with a friend. They were sharing a plate of fruit.

"What's that?" asked Suzy, curious.

"Melon," said her mum. "Would you like a piece?"

Suzy shook her head emphatically. "No!" she said. "I don't like it!"

"Suzy," said her mum, "how can you possibly say you don't like melon? You've never had it before. Try a piece, and then make up your mind. You can always spit it out if you really don't like the taste."

So Suzy tried a very small nibble. To her surprise, she discovered that melon is absolutely delicious. She ate half the plateful.

In the Bible, Psalm 34 says: "Taste and see that the Lord is good" (Psalm 34:8).

In an earlier chapter we looked at some of the many preconceived ideas people have about God. Maybe you have some of your own that haven't been put in this book.

But, if God is a Someone, not just a Something, then it should be possible to get to know God for yourself – to actually *meet* God in some way. All over the world there are people who say that this is indeed possible: you can talk to God, and God will listen; you can reach out to God, and make contact in a way you can feel. More than that: God is also talking *to you*! God is already reaching out to you.

When you think about it, it's no more of a big deal than Suzy tasting melon on that summer day for you to taste and see for yourself – to take a chance on God being real, and try an experiment. What do you have to lose?

So – how do you go about tasting God?

Discovering a sacred space

For years Paul has had in his study an old brown chair that he goes to sit in when he wants to take time to connect with God. As well as the chair in his study, there is a special place, on the Gower Peninsula in South Wales, which feels like a sacred space to him. It was there that he first encountered God in a significant, transformative way. It was there that he wrestled with the thought of leaving his regular job and giving his life to helping people discover wonderment and ask questions and explore faith. It is there that he returns every now and then when he has big stuff in his own life to tackle. It's there that he can really feel God near.

Have you got a special place like that, somewhere you could think of as a sacred space? A place near your home that you can easily get to – somewhere so beautiful it takes your breath away, or where your mind feels clear, and you can really think things through?

Many people say their sacred space is outside in the country – by the ocean, or walking in the woods or in the hills. But some people like to curl up somewhere quiet, maybe in their own bedroom, or in an old chair in the garden shed, with a cup of tea – and that's their Thinking Place, their sacred space.

When you find your sacred space, it's just a matter of getting comfortable and peaceful there, and saying what it is you want to say to God. Maybe: "God, if you are there, please make yourself known to me" – as simple as that! Or maybe there is something that is troubling you – an old hurt or a sense of injustice. You could talk to God about it honestly and openly, asking for help to understand and resolve what troubles your heart.

Talking to God in this way could be something you do on a regular basis – see what happens, see what you discover; look out for changes beginning in your life, both gradual and sudden.

Practising the presence of God

In seventeenth-century France, a young soldier called Nicholas Herman was badly injured fighting in the Thirty Years War. He worked as a servant in a big house for a while, and in middle age he felt drawn to try monastic life, and took the name Brother Lawrence at a big new monastery in Paris, where he became the cook. A gentle, cheerful person who didn't like a lot of fuss made of him, Brother Lawrence went quietly about his duties until his death in 1661. A small book – you can still buy it easily – was made from letters he had written and conversations he had had, explaining what he called "practising the presence of God", which describes how, wherever he was, whatever he was doing, he would just slip quietly into an awareness of God's presence, resting in God's friendship, companionable.

This short book (it's called *The Practice of the Presence of God*, and you can find it online, to read there or to buy a copy for yourself) is about something so simple, and yet it has completely changed the lives of many people. It's something about his gentleness – the book exudes peace, and you can feel the calm and strength that shone from Brother Lawrence's life.

You might like to read the book and have a try yourself at "practising the presence of God"; placing yourself in conscious awareness of a God who is quietly with you as you go about your ordinary daily tasks.

Reading the Bible

Although the Bible looks like just one big book, it's better described as a library of sixty-six books written over hundreds of years and all bound into one.

It contains different kinds of literature: stories and poems and accounts of visions, letters and songs, and books of law telling the ancient Jews how to structure their society.

Different people will always pick out different parts as their favourite, or as hard to understand. But many people find the four Gospels (Matthew, Mark, Luke and John) at the beginning of the New Testament a good place to start. The Old Testament is the part that relates to all the years before Jesus was born, and the New Testament is about the faith, teaching, life and impact of Jesus. "Gospel" means "good news". The Gospel of John is very beautiful and inspiring, and people often find that a helpful place to start.

You can even get the Bible on audio CD, so it's possible to listen to it in the car while you're driving, if that's more convenient for you. It is also available as a free app for your iPhone.

The Bible has often been described as a "living book", and people are sometimes amazed to find a phrase here and there that seems to stand out, speaking to them very personally and directly, touching with extraordinary relevance on some matter that is occupying their thoughts.

The Bible is a wise and honest book, and wherever you are in your own faith and thinking, there is lots in it to challenge and inspire you.

Finding a soul friend

When Paul made his first hesitant forays into spiritual country, a friend called Terry helpfully took him under his wing. Terry and his wife invited Paul to their home frequently. They would eat together and talk together. Paul found him an easy person to open up to, and he felt safe exploring his own puzzling questions with Terry. As Paul became curious to discover more, Terry invited him along to hear different speakers and meet other questioners and seekers. Terry was the man who took Paul to different spiritual events to broaden his experience.

Today, one of Paul's soul friends is Steve – this time more like a brother than a guide. They meet every couple of weeks to talk about how things are going in their lives – just ordinary things, or bigger dilemmas and decisions as they arise.

Paul has found it encouraging and supportive to have someone he can talk things through with. It can be easy to get into lazy ways of thinking, or see only one point of view, if you don't have a friend you can share with. Sometimes the perspective of another person brings a surprising shaft of light, a completely different approach.

Of course it's not always easy to find someone who can be a Terry or a Steve for us, but it's certainly worth making the effort to look. You may feel a sense of rapport with someone at a Puzzling Questions course; or if you can't think of anybody who would be right, it may be a way of trying out talking to God in your sacred space times: "Please will you help me find a soul friend?"

Making a "thank-you" box

Pearl was a teacher in a primary school all her working life. During that time she did some wonderful things with the children, but what they all remember is the "thank-you" box with the slot in its lid for them to post notes saying "thank you" for every good thing that happened to them. It was a habit Pearl had learned from her mother, who used to do the same thing at home.

At the end of each week, on Friday afternoon, Pearl would open the box, and let all the "thank yous" out. She would read them to the children, and together they would enjoy taking time to acknowledge that life is good, that people are kind, that happy moments come our way and that the world is full of beauty.

After a while, word got round about the thank-you box, and first one of the other teachers asked if Pearl would mind her class doing the same, and then the principal asked if it would be OK for the whole school to have a thank-you box, reading out the notes in school assembly once a week.

To nurture a thankful heart – an "attitude of gratitude", as they say – helps us to develop spiritually; a great soul is never unappreciative.

One way to "taste and see" the presence of God is to have two boxes – a "please" and a "thank-you". Into the "please" box go all the notes about things that need fixing – a friend is in trouble, a child is ill, a neighbour has marriage problems, a colleague has been made redundant. Think carefully and realistically about the help you would like to ask for that person, and write your request on a note to drop into the please box. Meanwhile, keep dropping your "thank yous" into the box marked for them. When a few weeks have gone by – a month maybe – open the boxes and read through the notes you have written. You may find that some of the "pleases" have turned into "thank yous". Write "THANK YOU" on them in big letters, and transfer them to the other box. Put the rest back to cook a bit longer. When you sit quietly in your sacred space, you may like to hold and turn over in your mind the things you have written down, and show them to the God you are tasting.

Being kind

This is an interesting one. How can being kind help you with puzzling questions?

In the book of Micah in the Bible there is a question about the way God wants us to live: "And what does the Lord require of you? To act justly and to love mercy and to walk humbly with your God" (Micah 6:8).

So, being fair and kind and not being arrogant are what the Bible says God is asking for. When you think about it, a lot of the things we object to in the world – things that make us angry with God or that even make us refuse to believe God exists at all – would simply go away by themselves if we all lived like that. War and poverty, and cruelty to children and animals, and greedy misuse of the world's resources – all those would just dry up and disappear if everybody on earth lived by that little verse in the book of Micah.

Being kind is a way of aligning ourselves with the flow of what is good – with what those who have a Christian world view refer to as "the will of God". It's like a way of tuning into the wavelength where the music is.

Conclusion

It's only a matter of opinion, but for many the best films are those that don't tie up all the loose ends by the time the final credits start rolling. In fact, sometimes the more loose ends there are, the greater the impact of the film and the conversation that follows.

These might be the romantic films that leave you asking the question "Will they or won't they get married?" In the genre of action movies the question we are sometimes asked to ponder is "Did he survive the crash or the explosion?" – maybe the fact that there is a sequel being advertised gives us a clue!

As we reach the close of this book our hope is that, rather than have a set of party-piece answers to some of life's more difficult questions, you have instead some newly formed and recently acknowledged questions that you can take forward with you. They might be different questions from those you started with; they might be questions that you have never thought about before, or they might be questions that are far more important to you. What is significant is that they are *your* questions and that they can form the basis for your future adventures.

We hope that you have picked up a little bit of information along the way and perhaps deepened your appreciation of the questions of life and the contexts in which these questions need to be considered, but our aim has primarily been to journey with you in beginning to explore these vast questions.

But what next? Rather than simply saying goodbye and wishing you well, we thought it might be useful to jot down a list of possible routes that you might consider taking.

Stepping stones

1. Do carry on talking to those with whom you have had conversations about these questions. If you have attended a Puzzling Questions course, then we would encourage you to talk further with the people you have come to know on the course or the people you came along with. As we mentioned, when talking about the spiritual realm, having a soul friend can make a very big difference to your spiritual journey.

2. For those who, having read the book or engaged in the course, would like to talk with those of us involved in putting together the *Puzzling Questions* book and course, we have a question-and-answer facility on the Puzzling Questions website. Go to www.puzzlingquestions.org.uk and then click on the relevant page.

3. As we noted in the Introduction, this book is part of a six-session course that aims to help people ponder some of life's difficult questions. Following the format of food–presentation–discussion, the course gives everyone who comes on it an opportunity to engage with these questions in the way that best suits them. Delegates on the course are given an opportunity to come along with friends or make new ones, to eat food together, to enjoy a simple presentation that aims to open up each question and then to gather with others to either listen to or engage in the conversations that follow. Information about the course (and how to register an interest in coming along to one or to see where the nearest one to you is) can be found on the Puzzling Questions website: www.puzzlingquestions.org.uk

4. For those who don't think they want to do the Puzzling Questions course next but would rather try something else, there are a number of other courses that are worth going on. Those who would like information about one of the other courses available, whether it is the well-known Alpha course or the highly stimulating Y course or the thoughtful Christianity Explored, or one of the many other useful courses available that help people think through the questions of life, can either use the search engine Google to obtain details or contact us via our website.

5. Have a look at Jesus. There are lots of different ways of digging up information about Jesus. You can visit the www.rejesus.com website, which is packed full of interesting information or buy/borrow some books that explore who this first-century magnet was. Or you might consider engaging with the Bible – a book that is crammed with material about Jesus and the claims he made about himself and the things he did while walking this earth. If you decide to go with reading or listening to the Bible, then start with either Mark or John.

Why might you want to find out more about Jesus? Many have discovered that the quality of his character marks him out as a unique figure. He was someone who managed to express all of the virtues that we aspire to. He was a truth-teller who managed to say what needed to be said in the way that best helped the people or person he was talking to. They might not always have bought into what he was saying, but their decision to opt out had nothing to do with the type of person he was. What is more, he was someone who always had time for people – he had a job, a mission that consumed him, and yet along the way you constantly find him deeply involved with those whom society had rejected.

Not only was he a remarkable person with regard to character, but what he said made masses of sense. Today, many people are more concerned about whether something works than about whether it is true. What Jesus presents is a pattern for life that is both: it works *and* it is true. It works whatever situation you find yourself in, whatever life throws at you, or whatever you have got yourself into. The wisdom Jesus gives, whether directly or through one of his followers, is relevant to how we do marriage or child-rearing, and how we work for the boss or treat the people we employ. Whatever stage of life you find yourself at, Jesus' teaching has a helpful relevance.

As those who have been created by God, we have been made to have spiritual encounters and experiences of God. What Jesus claims to be able to do is give us those adventures. As someone with a unique relationship to God – he claimed to be God's Son, who had been sent from God to help people reconnect with his Father – Jesus was keen to help people come into all that they were destined for. How he is able to do that is all a little bit complicated, but what many have personally discovered both during the course of his life and since is that what he has to say works.

Some might suggest that Jesus is himself the greatest puzzling question of all. He has made quite an impact on the history of the world. During his life on earth there were people who didn't believe his claims, those who wanted to get rid of him, and those who were prepared to give up everything to get to know him and become one of his followers. Those responses have been present throughout history. What type of person can have that diverse an impact on people?

What is it about Jesus that causes some people

to dismiss what he said about himself or about life? Why would individuals want to get rid of someone who encouraged people through his stories to care for others, and who went out of his way to make a real difference in the lives of those who desperately needed it? How on earth did he manage to inspire such devotion in people from all walks of life – a devotion that was in some instances very costly?

The question of Jesus is one that occupies the attention of every major world religion and has commanded the interest of the greatest philosophers and thinkers through the ages. There are many millions of people who find in Jesus the beginnings of an answer to the puzzling questions they are asking. Jesus might in the end be rejected by an individual, but the question about Jesus needs to be addressed by every thinking person. In the final verses of the Gospel of John there is a fascinating interaction between Jesus and the disciple whom we sometimes call Doubting Thomas. It might be good to leave the last word with this doubter who grappled with the ultimate Puzzling Question.

Eight days later the disciples were together again, and this time Thomas was with them. The doors were locked; but suddenly, as before, Jesus was standing among them. He said, "Peace be with you." Then he said to Thomas, "Put your finger here, and look at my hands. Put your hand into the wound in my side. Don't be faithless any longer. Believe!"

"My Lord and my God!" Thomas exclaimed.

John 20:26–31, NLT

Puzzling Questions: The course

This book is part of a six-session course that is being run all over the country.

These two-hour sessions give people an opportunity to ponder some of life's deeper questions.

Following the format of a shared meal, followed by a presentation, followed by a discussion, each session focuses on one of the six questions.

As part of each get-together you and your friends are given an opportunity to meet new people, enjoy some entertaining and informative presentations and engage in conversation about that session's topic.

Those who enjoy just listening are free, without pressure, to sit back and reflect on what others think. Those who enjoy a good chat have the opportunity to express their views and engage in discussion with others.

For more information about the course and where it is presently being run, or to read the feedback of others who have already participated, please visit www.puzzlingquestions.org.uk

or write to:

The Ugly Duckling Company
PO Box 31
Lydney
GL15 6YP

THE 8 SECRETS OF HAPPINESS
PAUL GRIFFITHS & MARTIN ROBINSON

The twenty-first century is a century of limitless possibilities. We are surrounded by innumerable products promising to make us more attractive, more healthy, more intelligent, more popular and more successful. But somehow, it's not quite enough – there's more to happiness than having a great job, designer clothes, a busy social life or a fat bank balance.

This book will guide you through the eight secrets which psychologists have discovered to be the foundations of happiness, revealing a hidden dimension they all share. In an age of unprecedented wealth, coupled with unprecedented unhappiness and even depression, this book is a wake-up call. It's time to rediscover happiness – and here's how.

ISBN 978 0 7459 5329 8   £7.99 UK

www.lionhudson.com/lion